America Unequal

America Unequal

Sheldon Danziger
and
Peter Gottschalk

Russell Sage Foundation
New York

Harvard University Press
Cambridge, Massachusetts
London, England

Library of Congress Cataloging-in-Publication Data

Danziger, Sheldon.
America unequal / Sheldon Danziger and Peter Gottschalk.
    p. cm.
Includes bibliographical references and index.
ISBN 0-674-01810-9 (cloth)
ISBN 0-674-01811-7 (pbk.)
1. Income distribution—United States. 2. Poverty—United States.
3. United States—Social policy. 4. Labor market—United States. 5. United
States—Economic policy. I. Gottschalk, Peter, 1942– . II. Title.
HC110.I5D329   1995
339.2′2′0973—dc20   95-11218
CIP

To Sandy and Barbara,
for years of support and encouragement

Acknowledgments

This research was made possible by a grant from the Russell Sage Foundation. Additional support was provided by the Presidential Initiatives Fund of the University of Michigan. Gregory Acs, Scott Allard, Maria Cancian, David Dickinson, Jon Haveman, Carol Kallman, Steve Pizer, and Deborah Reed provided valuable research assistance. Rebecca Blank, Maria Cancian, Edward Gramlich, Jeffrey Lehman, Sharon Parrott, Wendell Primus, Deborah Reed, Eugene Smolensky, and especially Robinson Hollister and Eric Wanner provided helpful comments on a previous draft. Louise Cunliffe and Michael Coble prepared the data extracts. Carol Crawford diligently typed multiple drafts. Camille Smith edited the manuscript; Elizabeth Gretz shepherded it through production.

Data in Table 7.1 are taken with permission from Henry S. Farber, "The Incidence and Costs of Job Loss: 1982–91," *Brookings Papers on Economic Activity: Microeconomics,* 1993, Table 1, p. 88. Figures 6.1 and 6.2 are plotted from data in Lynn A. Karoly, "The Trend in Income Inequality among Families, Individuals, and Workers in the United States," Table 2.B.2, in *Uneven Tides: Rising Inequality in America,* edited by Sheldon H. Danziger and Peter Gottschalk, © 1993 Russell Sage Foundation, used by permission of Russell Sage Foundation. Figure 7.3 is plotted from data in James Medoff, "Middle-Aged and Out-of-Work," Democratic Study Center Report Series, April 1993, Tables 4 and 5, used by permission.

Contents

America Unequal

Chapter 1

The Diminishing American Dream

Since the early 1970s, Americans have experienced hard economic times, times characterized by slow economic growth and increasing inequality in earnings and family incomes. The gaps between the incomes of the rich and the poor and between those of the rich and the middle class have been expanding. There have also been growing gaps among families within most demographic groups (for example, black families, married-couple families). Concerns about the American standard of living have received much attention from the media, academics, and political candidates, and have become central to debates about public policy.

The economic hardships faced by so many Americans represent a sharp break with our recent economic history. Family incomes, adjusted for inflation, doubled in the two decades after World War II, but they have grown very little in the past twenty years. Many workers now have lower real earnings—earnings adjusted for inflation—than they did in the 1970s. Earlier generations took the American dream for granted: each generation assumed it would have a higher standard of living than its parents. Today's young adults, in contrast, face diminished prospects. Many worry that they may never achieve their parents' current standard of living.

Their parents, today's mature workers and retirees, came of age in an entirely different economic climate. During the 1950s and 1960s most men were employed at jobs that paid "good wages," and more and more jobs provided health insurance and pensions. Inflation-adjusted wages rose steadily, and most men earned enough to support a family on one income. They were able to buy homes at relatively low prices and interest rates, accumulate wealth as the real value of their houses increased, and retire with Social Security benefits that had grown rapidly in real terms during their working lives.

This was an era during which the American dream was fulfilled for most families. The incomes of the rich, the poor, and the middle class all increased at similar rates. If some benefited more than others, they tended to be those who had started at a greater disadvantage, such as racial and ethnic minorities and those with little education. This rapid economic growth, coupled with a small drop in inequality of incomes over these two decades, reinforced the conventional wisdom that "a rising tide lifts all boats"—that in a healthy economy the rate of poverty would steadily fall. Indeed, the poverty rate was cut in half between the late 1940s and the early 1960s and cut in half again by the early 1970s.

The experience of the past two decades has been dramatically different. Many of the current generation of young workers lack the economic security of their parents. Their jobs pay relatively low wages. Fewer jobs now provide health insurance and private pensions. Both white-collar and blue-collar workers have higher rates of unemployment. In many families both husband and wife must work to support the family and to cover the higher costs of owning a home. For young workers, the retirement age has been raised to 67 and Social Security benefits will reflect a lower rate of return on their Social Security taxes than their parents received.

Most important, although the tide has risen slowly, it has become uneven and no longer lifts all boats. We see the recent period as one in which the large yachts, moored in the safe harbors, rose with the tide, while the small boats ran aground. No matter how it is measured, inequality in income, earnings, and wealth (Wolff, 1992) has increased over the past twenty years, and poverty has remained high.

This pattern was particularly strong during the 1980s and early 1990s. In contrast to the American dream, those whose incomes grew during this period were highly concentrated at the top of the income distribution. Inequality widened both between demographic groups and within them. The most disadvantaged benefited least: the young gained less than the old; less-educated workers gained less than more-educated workers; single-parent families gained less than two-parent families; blacks and Hispanics gained less than whites. Poverty remained high and inequality of earnings and of family income increased.

Economic hardship is more widespread than many Americans realize. There is a popular tendency to focus on inner-city poverty or single-mother families or displaced factory workers and to attribute poverty primarily to their lack of work effort or of skills. But in the 1980s and early 1990s inequality increased within most broader groups of the population as well. That is, while, on average, white-collar workers fared better than blue-collar workers and married couples fared better than mother-only families, many white-collar workers and many workers in married-couple families were also laid off or had lower real earnings.

Inequality increased even among the most-advantaged groups. For example, college graduates earn much more than less-educated workers, and their earnings grew much faster than the earnings of other workers in the 1980s. Nonetheless, in today's turbulent labor market, a college degree does not guarantee high wages, as many young graduates also face economic hardship. In 1991, 16 percent of male and 26 percent of female college graduates (those without post-college degrees) between the ages of 25 and 34 worked at some time during the year but earned less than the poverty line for a family of four ($13,924). In 1973 the corresponding percentages were 11 percent for men and 37 percent for women.[1]

Powerful economic forces have diminished the economic prospects of millions of Americans and caused rising hardship and poverty. Employers have reduced their demand for less-skilled and less-experienced workers. As a result, and through no fault of their own, millions of workers have more difficulty finding jobs. And many of the available jobs offer lower real wages and benefits than similar jobs two decades ago.

Our analysis challenges the view, emphasized during the 1994 congressional elections, that restraining government social spending and reforming welfare should be America's top domestic policy priorities. Rather, as we will argue, the major domestic priority should be to address an economic environment that has been hostile toward less-skilled workers since the early 1970s.

The effects of recessions on family income are quite evident. Unemployment rises sharply and earnings decline rapidly. The effects of the slow economic growth and rising inequality of the last two decades, however, were less visible, as job prospects slowly eroded and wage increases lagged behind the inflation rate. This may explain why Americans tend to cite the behavior of the disadvantaged, rather than the economic changes that have made it so hard for millions to make ends meet, as the primary cause of poverty. The poor and the middle class have fared so badly because of an erosion of their labor market opportunities, not because of an erosion of their work ethic.

The contrasts between the two economic eras—the rising tides of the post–World War II economic boom and the slow growth and uneven tides of the past two decades—first emerged after the 1973 oil embargo. The resulting price shock and the recession of 1974–1975 marked the beginning of a decade of both high unemployment and high inflation. For most Americans the steady postwar improvement in living standards came to an end. President Carter was blamed for the rising misery index—a concept developed by Arthur Okun: the sum of the unemployment and inflation rates—and President Reagan was elected to "get the economy moving again." In hindsight, it is clear that the origins of today's economic hardships can be found in the early 1970s. But this was clearly not the view in the early 1980s.

The Reagan administration painted the 1970s as a period of temporary economic difficulties brought about by the OPEC cartel and Democratic mismanagement of the economy. As the recession came to an end late in 1982 and a long recovery began, optimism about the prospects for raising living standards for all Americans reappeared. For example, Martin Anderson (1990), one of President Reagan's White House policy advisers, labeled the recovery of the 1980s "the greatest consistent burst of economic activity ever seen in the U.S." That recovery did last for more than seven years. This was an unusually long expansion, rivaling that of the 1960s, which lasted for more than eight years. But, as we will document, the recovery of the 1980s was unusual in that only a small portion of the population benefited. The recovery did lead to significant growth in the number of jobs, falling rates of unemployment and inflation, and increases in the gross national product (GNP). Despite the higher aggregate employment and earnings, however, millions of families continued to experience economic hardship.

For most of the post–World War II era, shrinking unemployment rates and growing GNP were associated with rising living standards for all Americans. This association broke down during the 1980s. The coincidence of a growing economy and continuing hardship for millions of families set the stage for both a change in academic thinking about the level and distribution of living standards and a change in presidential administrations. The issue of *fairness* moved from the background to center stage in the early 1990s.

In the early 1980s, when we began writing about rising inequality and high poverty rates, these topics were of interest mainly to academics (Gottschalk and Danziger, 1984, 1985). There was disagreement as to whether the trends we noted were anything more than temporary outcomes of the two recessions that occurred in 1980 and 1981–1982. Many analysts (for example, Blank and Blinder, 1986) expected that after the Federal Reserve's tight monetary policy brought inflation under control the economy would resume the type of balanced growth that had characterized most of the postwar years. They took it for granted that, as the economy continued to recover, most Americans—the poor and the middle class as well as the rich—would again experience real growth in earnings and family incomes.

Research on poverty and inequality intensified through the 1980s and took center stage by the early 1990s. There was some discussion during the 1988 presidential campaign of the growing gaps between the rich and the poor and between the rich and the middle class. However, because the economic recovery was still in progress, popular discussion emphasized the still-rising aggregate level of economic activity and the falling rates of unemployment and inflation. As long as the economy kept growing, there was hope that those who had not yet shared in the gains from the recovery would eventually benefit. The fairness issue did arise sporadically during the late 1980s, but it tended to be equated with partisan politics. Democrats pointed to the widening gaps between the haves and the have-nots; Republicans emphasized "the longest peacetime expansion in history" and argued that everyone was better off in a growing, low-inflation economy.

The recovery of the 1980s and the Reagan administration's optimistic focus on the growth of average living standards are now distant memories to politicians, the press, and the public. The recession of 1990–1991 changed the economic situation, but popular opinion shifted even more dramatically. Kevin Phillips, a political analyst, recounted the divergence in economic fortunes of the poor, the middle class, and the rich in his best-seller *The Politics of Rich and Poor* (1990). Increasingly, in the 1990s, a revisionist view of the 1980s took hold as many Americans realized they were not any better off than they had been in the late 1970s or early 1980s.

This perception was brought home as major corporations continued downsizing and laid off many more white-collar workers than in previous recessions. During the 1992 presidential campaign, a Republican president was blamed for our economic troubles. The Bush administration was criticized for relying on "trickle-down economics" that had not benefited most workers during the 1980s, and for not acting more aggressively to offset the effects of the 1990–1991 recession. President Clinton was elected to spur growth in employment and to help those who "worked harder for lower wages."

Nonetheless, corporate restructuring and additional layoffs continued during the economic recovery of the early 1990s. Numerous articles in the media documented the economic hardships faced by young college graduates (Lewin, 1994), by middle-aged, college-educated middle managers (Uchitelle, 1994), and by those who had lost high-paying manufacturing jobs and had been re-employed at lower wages, often without pensions or health insurance (Johnson, 1994).

Voters' dissatisfaction with their economic prospects contributed to another electoral change in 1994. Even though during 1993 and 1994 the economy gained strength, inflation remained low, and the unemployment rate dropped, the public opted for another shift in economic policy and elected a Republican majority in Congress. As a result, both President Clinton and the Republicans proposed tax relief for the middle class as a major goal for 1995. While the President still defended social programs for the poor, however, the Republicans sought dramatic reductions in antipoverty spending.

In our view, the slow growth in American living standards and the rising inequality in incomes result primarily from structural economic changes that have evolved over the past two decades. We will not resolve our economic problems by voting one political party or the other out of office or by making small changes in policy. We will not restore the American dream for the middle class by spending less on behalf of the poor. Such cuts will merely push the poor further outside the economic mainstream.

Recessions and Recoveries

As we have said, our current economic problems emerged in the early 1970s. Frank Levy (1987) labeled the decade 1973–1982 the "quiet depression." During that period, median family income fell and poverty increased. With regard to growth in average family income, the quiet depression did come to an end with the recovery of the 1980s. For most younger workers and for many workers without college degrees, however, it has continued unabated.

Although the economic recovery of the 1980s lasted longer than most recoveries, its effects on living standards were modest. It is understandable that the mere fact that the economy was finally moving forward again after a period of unprecedented unemployment and inflation could evoke optimism. The unemployment rate, after reaching almost 10 percent during the 1981–1982 recession, fell to about 5.5 percent by the late 1980s, and inflation fell from the low teens at the end of the 1970s to less than 5 percent in the late 1980s.

From a longer-run perspective, however, the growth of living standards was disappointing. The income growth during the 1980s followed a decade in which real family income fell—even for married couples, despite the larger numbers of wives in the labor force. Furthermore, even by the mid-1990s many families whose real incomes did grow experienced their gains primarily because of increased work effort, especially by wives. In contrast to the 1950s and 1960s, when men's earnings grew rapidly, the earnings of married men increased relatively little from the mid-1970s to the mid-1990s. In addition, a smaller percentage of men earned enough to support a family with only their own paychecks (Acs and Danziger, 1993; U.S. Bureau of the Census, 1992b).

In this context, the entire period 1973–1993 was remarkable. Real median family income in the early 1990s was only slightly above its 1973 level. An American generation had experienced only a modest increase in its average standard of living, and economic inequality and insecurity had increased.

Long-run trends in consumer confidence mirror these long-run trends in living standards. Each month since 1951 the University of Michigan's Institute for Social Research has asked a representative sample of Americans about their expectations concerning their own finances and the course of the national economy over the next one to five years. The responses are converted into an index of consumer confidence. The index averaged about 95 in the 1950s and 1960s, fell to an average of 71 in the 1970s, and rose only modestly to 79 in the 1980s.[2] Furthermore, in the early 1990s most people under age 45 considered their financial situation to be worse than that of their parents at the same age, while those over 45 considered themselves better off than their parents (Uchitelle, 1993).

This lack of consumer confidence undoubtedly reflects the increased economic hardship that many Americans have experienced despite the moderate growth in average incomes. Since the recession of 1973–1975, poverty rates have risen more during each recession than they have fallen during each ensuing recovery. As a result, poverty rates have become detached from economic growth. If growth in family income had been evenly shared among all income groups, poverty in the early 1990s would have been somewhat below its 1973 level. But growth was uneven. Poverty rates fell somewhat after the recession of 1981–1982, but the official poverty rate for all persons in the early 1990s remained substantially higher than it had been in 1973. The official poverty rate for 1992 was 14.5 percent, about the same as in 1966 and 1967. If the poverty rate in 1992 had been at its 1973 level—11.1 percent—almost 9 million fewer Americans would have been poor.

At the top end of the income distribution, the "haves" benefited much more than their fellow citizens. During the 1980s their earnings and property income went up and their federal income tax rates went down. While the poverty rate remained high in the 1980s, the percentage of the population that could be classified as rich increased rapidly. Indeed, the ranks of the rich reached an all-time high. (We define the rich as those families with incomes greater than seven times the poverty line; see Chapter 3.) While the average American was somewhat better off in the early 1990s, those at the top had never had it so good.

The Public Policy Dilemma

The failure of the poverty rate to fall back to the levels achieved two decades earlier despite modest economic growth and increased average family income, together with the dramatic divergence in the experiences of the haves and the have-nots, has stimulated debate among academics, the press, and policymakers about the economic polarization of American society and about potential public and private remedies.

There is now a great deal of agreement as to why inequality in earnings and family income increased. Most of the increase can be attributed to technological changes, the globalization of markets, and other structural changes in the economy that created more demand for higher-skilled relative to lower-skilled workers. Younger workers, blue-collar workers, and those without college degrees all fared badly in the changing labor market. There is little agreement in policy circles, however, on how to counter these market-generated hardships. One approach is to focus primarily on macro-economic targets and changes in average living standards, with the hope that the poor, as well as the rich and the middle class, will benefit. The alternative is to use tax and social policies to offset the economic hardships generated in the labor market.

Our goal is to document how economic, demographic, and public policy changes have affected the level and distribution of income over the past forty-five years. An understanding of these historical experiences will provide the basis for our evaluation of economic and antipoverty policies intended to reduce poverty and inequality in the years ahead. We address such specific questions as these: Why have poverty rates remained so high? Why have the gaps between the rich and the poor and between the rich and the middle class grown so wide in recent years? Why didn't the gains of the 1980s trickle down more to the middle class and the disadvantaged? What changes have made more of the population rich without reducing poverty? What can be done to reduce poverty and the economic inequalities that have widened over the past two decades?

We will find our answers by contrasting the effects of economic growth and public policies in the past two decades with those in the two decades after World War II. Reviewing a great deal of evidence concerning changes in the level and distribution of American living standards over the past four decades, we will show that the growing gaps between the rich and the poor and the rich and the middle class are relatively new economic phenomena. We will also challenge the widely held view that economic growth in itself will both benefit the average American family and solve the problems of poverty and economic hardship in our affluent society.

The evidence we present demonstrates that economic, demographic, and policy changes have rendered obsolete the view that economic growth is the major factor determining how many people are rich and how many are poor. There is no evidence to suggest that we can grow our way out of the problems that have hurt so many families. It is no longer true that "almost all of the variation in the poverty rate is tracked by movements in median family income" (Ellwood and Summers, 1986, p. 81). If increased inequality in the distribution of economic rewards is as central to an understanding of poverty and economic hardship as we believe it is, then stimulating economic growth and avoiding recessions are necessary, but not sufficient, solutions to America's poverty problem. Of course, the problems of poverty and income inequality cannot be remedied in the absence of economic growth. Indeed, economic efficiency and full employment should remain important goals for the economy.

But distributional considerations should not be neglected, as they were during the 1980s.

A call for greater government involvement in policies concerning the labor market and poverty, however, does not tell us how much more society should provide, how the funds should be spent, or how the revenues should be raised. Economists have long recognized that redistributive policies may lead to losses in efficiency, particularly to reductions in work effort or savings. In addressing this trade-off between efficiency and equity, Alan Blinder was eloquent, if not precise, when he concluded that "what this country needs now in the realm of income distribution policy is exactly what it needs, and has often been unable to get, in so many other problem areas: An economic policy with a hard head and a soft heart. A hard head to remind us of the wondrous efficiency of the marketplace, and how foolish it is to squander this efficiency without good reason. And a soft heart to remind us that championing the cause of society's underdogs has long been, and remains, one of the noblest functions of government" (1982, p. 30; see also Blinder, 1987).

When Blinder wrote this, most analysts would have predicted that even without a soft heart, a seven-year economic expansion would greatly reduce poverty. The experience of the 1980s, however, revealed such expectations as illusions. We have not been able to grow our way out of America's high poverty rates. If, by the year 2000, we are to have poverty rates as low as those now common in Canada and most Western European countries, a soft-hearted but hard-headed antipoverty strategy is essential.

Our concern with the entire income distribution is not an attack on the rich. We do not propose restraining the incomes of the rich merely to reduce inequality. Rather, we examine why the incomes of the poor and the middle class have grown so slowly relative to those of the rich, why inequality has increased even between workers with similar education and skills, and what government can do to help those who have not benefited from the economic growth of recent years.[3]

Robert Lampman, one of the key architects of the official measure of poverty, emphasizes that the poverty line reflects a concern about "a national minimum—an income level for each family size below which we do not want any American to have to live" (1971, p. 49). He goes on to note that the declaration of an antipoverty goal involved a rejection of any specific goal for reducing income inequality. President Johnson sought to raise the incomes of the poor and not to reduce the incomes of the rich. Lampman argues that American social policy should not primarily be aimed at restraining the incomes of the rich, as this would reduce inequality but not poverty or economic hardship.

We agree that reducing poverty by raising the incomes of the poor and of low-wage workers should be the top policy priority. However, it is difficult to envision a policy that could raise the incomes of these groups without in some way financing the programs through increased taxation of the wealthy. With this sort of policy, after taking account of taxes and government transfers, the gains for the poor and low-income workers and the taxation of the rich would lower both poverty and inequality.

An important conclusion of our analysis of the experience of the past forty-five years is that economic and social policies cannot be pursued as if they represented independent realms. To this day, there is a tendency to see the falling real wages of less-educated workers and the slow growth in the living standards of the middle class as unconnected to the problems of the unemployed, the working poor, welfare recipients, and the inner-city "underclass." The popular view that anyone who works hard can get ahead in America is still so widely held that it fosters the myth that most who remain poor or do not get ahead must be personally responsible for their plight.

In fact, some trends in behavior, such as increases in out-of-wedlock childbearing, divorce, and participation in illegal activities, are serious social problems that contribute to the high poverty rate. But their role is small compared with that of the major economic trend of the past two decades—the slow growth in living standards that bypassed so many families. This period has been a time of economic distress for the middle class, the working poor, the unemployed, welfare recipients, and the underclass alike. The United States has experienced a continuum of economic hardship that has kept some from achieving the living standard they expected and others from achieving even a poverty-line standard. To return to our favorite metaphor, all these groups have been affected by the same economic tidal wave.

The factory workers' children who graduate from high school in the mid-1990s cannot expect to receive the kind of wages and benefits their fathers earned when they graduated from high school and were hired by large manufacturing firms in the early 1970s. And the corporate managers' children who graduate from college today can no longer expect the secure employment and opportunities for promotion that their fathers enjoyed. Indeed, as we noted, both young high school graduates and young college graduates in the labor market of the early 1990s are more likely than were similar graduates two decades ago to earn less than the poverty line for a family of four. Today's young workers are also likely to face longer spells of unemployment than their fathers did.

As we will document, it was the economy that generated unequal fortunes and diminished prospects. Contrary to the assertions of conservative social critics (Murray, 1984; Mead, 1992; Magnet, 1993), these problems were not primarily caused by well-intentioned government social policies that distorted the work ethic and family behavior of program participants. The poor are not turning away from the economy; rather, the economy has pulled away from the poor. If the average standard of living had doubled over the past two decades, and if that rising living standard had been widely shared by the poor, the middle class, and the rich, as in the two decades after World War II, then Lampman's 1971 prediction that poverty, as officially defined, would disappear by 1980 would have been fulfilled. However, given the experience of the past two decades and supposing that current economic, demographic, and public policy trends persist, we do not expect that goal to be reached by the year 2000. Poverty remains high today, and inequality has increased, not because of a failure of social policy or of personal responsibility, but because of a failure of the economy to perform as it did in the past.

While the problems of poverty and inequality have worsened, there are no simple villains to blame. The economic changes that have hurt so many families have been largely independent of economic and social policies. Conservatives blame inept government policies, and liberals blame the laissez-faire policies and programs of the Reagan-Bush years. But neither side addresses the central issue, that—unbeknownst to many analysts until quite recently and still unbeknownst to many policymakers—the national and international economic environment has been generating increased economic hardship and inequality among American workers since the early 1970s.

These structural economic changes, which have also occurred in many other industrialized countries, are the primary cause of the persistently high poverty rate and the rising inequality of the past two decades. There is a natural tendency, especially in the political arena, to find a single cause and to personalize the problem. Such efforts are counterproductive. This is not to say that policies are blameless. Indeed, the tax cuts of the early 1980s contributed to rising inequality, and the budget cuts to rising poverty (Gramlich, Kasten, and Sammartino, 1993). Nonetheless, changes in the labor market would have brought increased economic hardship even if tax and social welfare policies had remained as they were in 1980.

Rather than look backward, we must look toward the future and determine how the public and private sectors can adapt to these changes in the economic environment so as to reduce poverty and income inequality. As we will show, such adaptations will require a fundamental rethinking of a variety of public and private policies. The effort required will be considerable, but because millions of Americans are at risk of suffering economic hardship, it is vital to our nation's economic health. It is time to make the reduction of poverty once again a top national priority.

Chapter 2

Public Policies since the War on Poverty

Just as American standards of living have been dramatically altered by major structural changes in the economy, the public's goals for and expectations of antipoverty policies have changed as well. In the 1960s President Johnson declared the War on Poverty, and government antipoverty programs and policies were expanded. During the early 1980s these same programs and policies were the primary targets of President Reagan's budget retrenchment. By the late 1980s, as the public became increasingly aware that many Americans had not benefited from the long economic recovery, Congress cautiously expanded policies designed to combat poverty. And President Clinton, early in his administration, reemphasized antipoverty policies and sought to introduce universal health insurance, promote employment for welfare recipients, increase subsidies for the working poor, and expand employment and training efforts—although Congress rejected many of his proposals. By 1994 public opinion had shifted again, and a Republican Congress proposed sweeping reductions in social spending.

Changes in public policy have been influenced by economic changes and, in turn, have reinforced the effects of those economic changes on poverty and inequality. The War on Poverty and Great Society programs were introduced and expanded during the economic boom of the 1960s. Both the growing economy and the expanded public programs contributed to further declines in poverty and income inequality.

During the economic expansion of the 1980s, however, when modest growth did not trickle down to the poor and the middle class, government assistance for the poor and the unemployed was scaled back. As a result, both economic changes and public policies contributed to increasing hardship. In the late 1980s Congress passed several policy changes intended to offset some of the negative effects of the slow economic growth and rising inequality. This brief renaissance of antipoverty policy ended as the Republican majority took control of Congress in January 1995. It is too early to judge how the proposed reductions of antipoverty efforts together with the modest economic growth of the early 1990s will affect poverty and inequality.

The Origins of the War on Poverty

Elements of the two basic strategies for attacking poverty and reducing income disparities—income transfers and employment programs—have been in place since the 1930s, when the Social Security system and a variety of work relief programs were established during Franklin D. Roosevelt's presidency. The elimination of poverty, however, was not an explicit goal of public policy at that time. Roosevelt's New Deal was focused on meeting the immediate needs of the unemployed. "Federal relief efforts were conceived, implemented, and politically sold as strictly temporary measures" (Heclo, 1986, p. 314). Although there was little commitment to eliminating poverty as such, the Social Security Act of 1935 established the major social programs that are still in operation—Social Security, unemployment compensation, and Aid to Families with Dependent Children.

After World War II the federal government explicitly adopted a goal of full employment, but not an antipoverty goal. Poverty was seen as primarily an effect of unemployment: if the unemployed could get jobs in the expanding postwar economy, they would not be poor. Thus it was thought that if macroeconomic policies could lower the unemployment rate, reductions in poverty would follow.

Contemporary policy concerns about poverty were first raised by John F. Kennedy after he visited poor areas of West Virginia during his presidential campaign. John Kenneth Galbraith's *The Affluent Society* (1958) with its chapter entitled "The New Position of Poverty"; Harry Caudill's portrait of Appalachian poverty in *Night Comes to the Cumberlands* (1963); and especially Michael Harrington's *The Other America* (1962) were all influential in making poverty a political issue for the Kennedy administration (Schlesinger, 1967). In the summer of 1963, at the same time that he was advocating a tax cut designed to reduce unemployment, Kennedy encouraged Walter Heller, then chairman of the Council of Economic Advisers (CEA), to analyze the problem of poverty and develop antipoverty programs. An analysis by Robert Lampman (1959), a member of the Council's staff, concluded that although poverty had been declining since 1947, the rate of decline had slowed since 1956. Lampman documented the need for explicit antipoverty policies; he found that high levels of employment and economic growth were essential but would not, on their own, substantially reduce poverty.

After President Kennedy was assassinated, President Johnson pushed forward various proposals to aid those with low incomes. In his first State of the Union address in January 1964 he declared the War on Poverty. Shortly thereafter he sent to Congress the 1964 *Economic Report of the President*, which included the first official analysis of poverty. This important document presented the conceptual foundation on which the War on Poverty was based.

The report listed a broad range of policy goals to reduce poverty: maintaining high employment, accelerating economic growth, fighting discrimination, improving regional economies, rehabilitating urban and rural communities, improving labor markets, expanding educational opportunities, providing more job opportunities for youth, improving health, promoting adult education and training, and assisting the aged and disabled. The writers of the report recognized the complexity of the problem of poverty and cautioned that no single program could meet all the needs of the poor.

The comprehensiveness of the strategies listed in the report signaled a reorientation of all domestic policies toward a concern with poverty. Robert Lampman (1974) later argued that the very declaration of the War on Poverty had an almost immediate and lasting effect, requiring the reassessment of all existing programs and new proposals in light of the question, "What does it do for the poor?" According to one of Johnson's biographers, "What had been largely the concern of a small number of liberal intellectuals and government bureaucrats became within six months the national disgrace that shattered the complacency of a people who had always considered their country a land of equal opportunity for all" (Goodwin, 1976, p. 188).

The conventional wisdom at that time was optimistic: if stable economic growth could be maintained, as it had been since the end of World War II, government could solve the problem of poverty if it devoted sufficient intellectual and financial resources to the task. President Johnson's analysts assumed that the economy would continue to grow, but recognized that economic growth could not serve as the sole antipoverty policy. Johnson declared: "We cannot and need not wait for the gradual growth of the economy to lift this forgotten fifth of our Nation above the poverty line . . . We know what must be done, and this Nation of abundance can surely afford to do it" (1964, p. 15). This economic optimism was warranted, as the economy had grown rapidly and consistently during the two decades after World War II and living standards had increased dramatically for wealthy, middle-class, and poor families alike.

Expanding Social Welfare Programs

Critics of the War on Poverty often charge that its primary strategy was "throwing money at the problem." But this was clearly not the case. Providing "a hand up and not a handout" was at the core of the policies. Education and training programs were considered the most important means for reducing poverty.

In its 1964 *Economic Report of the President*, the Council of Economic Advisers rejected a "cash" solution to poverty among the able-bodied, nonelderly poor: "this solution would leave untouched most of the roots of poverty. Americans want to earn the American standard of living by their own efforts and contributions. It will be far better, even if more difficult, to equip and to permit the poor of the Nation to produce and to earn the additional $11 billion, and more. We can surely afford greater generosity in relief of distress. But the major thrust of our campaign must be against causes rather than symptoms. We can afford the cost of that campaign too" (pp. 77–78).[1]

Expansion of employment and training programs was a major focus of policymakers' attention. The 1962 Manpower Development and Training Act (MDTA) was the first large-scale federal employment and training program since the Great Depression. It was intended to retrain unemployed workers displaced by technological change (Levitan and Taggart, 1976). MDTA was amended shortly after declaration of the War on Poverty to focus on disadvantaged persons, especially new entrants to the labor force with poor job skills—minorities, welfare recipients, low-income youth, and other hard-to-employ groups. It was augmented by the basic skills and training programs, such as the Job Corps, established under the Office of Economic Opportunity (OEO). Expenditures on programs for education, employment, and training increased rapidly during the late 1960s, but it never accounted for more than about one-quarter of federal antipoverty spending (Burtless, 1994).

While the War on Poverty sought to target resources on the poor, the goals of the Great Society were broader. They included, according to the 1965 *Economic Report of the President*, meeting the challenge of urbanization, educating citizens, raising health standards, and assuring equality of opportunity. A central focus was the reduction of discrimination against, and the enhancement of opportunity for, minorities and the disadvantaged. In addition, improvements in the physical and social environment were expected to benefit all citizens.

The goals of the Great Society called for various political and legal changes, especially in the realm of civil rights, along with those in the economic arena. Unprecedented social legislation expanded the scope of the American social welfare system and brought the federal government into areas previously reserved for state and local governments or the private sector.

The years 1964–1968 saw a major expansion of social welfare programs, unlike anything since the 1930s, and unlike anything in the subsequent twenty-five years. Legislative highlights included the Food Stamp Act of 1964, which provided coupons to be used when buying food;[2] the Equal Opportunity Act of 1964, which established the Office of Economic Opportunity (OEO) and its anti-poverty programs; the Elementary and Secondary Education Act of 1965, which targeted funds to poor school districts; the Head Start program, which focused on disadvantaged preschool children; and the 1965 Amendments to the Social Security Act, which established Medicare and Medicaid. While the rate of new legislation would slow after this first explosion, the number and size of social welfare and human capital programs continued to grow over the next decade.

During the decade following declaration of the War on Poverty, there was a willingness to experiment with new policies. For example, in the early 1970s Congress responded quickly to rising unemployment by expanding the length of time laid-off workers could receive unemployment compensation and by enacting a series of public service employment programs (PSE). The Emergency Employment Act (EEA), passed in 1971 as the unemployment rate reached 6 percent, authorized a two-year program to fund jobs with state and local governments.

While relatively small and focused on aggregate unemployment rather than on the disadvantaged, the EEA set the stage for the consolidation of job-creation strategies under the 1973 Comprehensive Employment and Training Act (CETA). CETA provided the administrative umbrella for federal employment and training and job-creation strategies between 1973 and 1982. PSE jobs were funded by the federal government, but were administered by hundreds of state and local government units and nonprofit organizations. The work ranged from child care to police and fire protection and was intended to provide transitional employment for the unemployed and the underemployed. The number of PSE participants increased from about 150,000 in 1972 to more than 750,000 in 1978, representing about 12.5 percent of all those unemployed at that time (Mirengoff et al., 1980).

PSE programs were more popular in Congress and with the public than cash assistance programs because they provided a hand up to the able-bodied. Nonetheless, they came under critical scrutiny as CETA expanded. For example, the autonomy given local governments in administering CETA employment allowed many programs to hire more highly skilled workers. Enrollees with previous job experience were often hired because they were more productive to the agency, even if the disadvantaged would have benefited more from the employment opportunity. In reaction, the 1976 amendments to CETA required that disadvantaged workers—long-term, low-income unemployed or welfare recipients—be given higher priority in public service employment.

At the same time, there was a shift in emphasis away from the direct provision of public service employment back to training programs. Critics of the shift argued that either there would not be sufficient jobs for the newly trained workers or they would displace other trained workers, but the policy mood in the late 1970s would not support increased government employment. The number of PSE jobs was cut from 750,000 in 1978 to 328,000 in 1980, even before President Reagan, who adamantly opposed direct efforts to create public jobs, entered the White House.

Spending on all social welfare programs increased dramatically between 1965 and 1975, more than doubling from 4.7 to 10.1 percent of the GNP. Spending on assistance for the poor and on education and training programs (included in the above totals) increased from 1.4 to 3.5 percent of GNP. In addition to the new programs, benefit levels increased in existing Social Security and welfare programs.[3]

About half of the total increase in social spending was accounted for by the introduction of Medicare and Medicaid and increased Social Security benefits. The increased social spending, together with the robust economic boom of the 1960s, seemed to fulfill the optimistic vision of the planners of the War on Poverty: the poverty rate, as officially measured, fell from 19 percent of all persons in 1964 to 11 percent in 1973.

This coincidence of rising social spending, a robust economy, and falling poverty led Robert Lampman (1971) and James Tobin (1967), two of President Johnson's key economic advisers on antipoverty initiatives, to forecast the elimination of poverty, as officially measured, by 1980. Unfortunately, as we will document in Chapter 3, the nation's uneven economic performance after the 1973 oil price shock and the severe recession of 1974–1975 brought progress against poverty (except among the elderly) to a halt.

The slowing economic growth and the rising unemployment of the late 1970s and early 1980s triggered doubts about the ability of government policies to control cyclical or structural unemployment and to reduce poverty. Disillusionment with government employment and training programs had several causes. First, evaluations of these programs suggested that they produced only mixed results. Second, unemployment rates more than doubled over the decade, despite substantial increases in federal spending on employment and training. Third, the objectives of many programs were not clearly stated, and this allowed critics to measure progress against other objectives and to give the programs low marks in meeting those goals. For example, programs that were designed to change the composition of the unemployed—that is, to lower unemployment among specific groups of workers—may have succeeded in meeting this limited goal even if they were unable to reduce the total number of unemployed.

At the same time that the unemployment rate rose despite increased government spending on employment and training programs, the poverty rate rose despite increased spending on cash assistance programs. The War on Poverty was intended to provide a hand up so that the poor could earn their way out of poverty. But the monthly AFDC caseload increased from about 4 million persons in 1964 to about 11 million for most of the 1970s.

These changes led many to question the entire antipoverty effort. As we will show, however, the rising rates of poverty and unemployment of the late 1970s and early 1980s were primarily caused by adverse economic conditions following the oil price shock of 1973. In hindsight, the relative stability in the poverty rate during the 1970s indicates that the social welfare programs and policies of the War on Poverty and the Great Society were at least partially successful in offsetting the effects of these adverse changes in the economy. If government spending on social programs had not continued to increase, poverty would have grown even more (see also Danziger and Gottschalk, 1985; Danziger and Weinberg, 1994).

Rising inflation in the late 1970s drove up federal income taxes, increased the cost of government programs, and eroded middle-class living standards. As a result, much of the public came to believe that government in general, and antipoverty programs in particular, had become too large. The optimistic vision of the War on Poverty planners that government could solve social problems was replaced by the pessimistic vision that government was "the problem" and that "throwing money" at social problems was no way to solve them. Some critics even argued that the antipoverty programs themselves were responsible for the continuing high rate of poverty and a variety of other economic and social ills (Murray, 1984). This view was widely held even though most of the increased social spending after the War on Poverty was targeted on the elderly, for whom the poverty rate had steadily declined throughout the 1970s.

The Reagan Retrenchment

The election of Ronald Reagan and a Republican Senate in 1980 gave those who believed that government was the problem an opportunity to reverse the course of economic and social policies. The President promoted supply-side economics and sought to reduce government programs in many areas. He singled out antipoverty programs for special attention: "In 1964, the famous War on Poverty was declared. And a funny thing happened. Poverty, as measured by dependency, stopped shrinking and then actually began to grow worse. I guess you could say 'Poverty won the War.' Poverty won, in part, because instead of helping the poor, government programs ruptured the bonds holding poor families together" (Reagan, 1986).

In his first budget, President Reagan called for an across-the-board reduction in personal income tax rates, a substantial increase in the defense budget, and "a drastic fiscal retrenchment" to reduce government spending, especially on social programs. He sought to reverse the priorities of the previous fifteen years, during which the federal budget had consumed an increasing percentage of GNP and its composition had shifted away from defense spending and toward social spending. Much of this agenda was successfully enacted in 1981. Several aspects of those changes in policy hurt poor and low-income families.

The reductions in income tax rates decreed by the Economic Recovery Tax Act of 1981 created such large deficits that since that time it has been very difficult to finance expansions in social programs. In an effort to broaden support in Congress, the White House and congressional leaders expanded the tax cuts beyond the administration's proposed rate reductions to include numerous additional incentives for business and investment. The reduction in revenues, first proposed as $450 billion over three years, was more than $700 billion over three years in the final act (Steuerle, 1991). As a result of this larger tax cut and the rapid increase in defense spending, the federal deficit more than tripled. The deficits led Congress to adopt a number of budgetary rules in the early 1990s that made it more difficult to fund new programs or expand social spending. The deficits, which are expected to persist into the next century, have continued to constrain new initiatives in the areas of antipoverty assistance and education, job training, and employment programs (see Chapter 8).

A direct shortcoming of the 1981 tax cuts was that they did not provide tax relief to low-income families. Although legislated rate reductions were 23 percent across the board, the standard deduction and the personal exemption were not increased. The amount of income taxes owed by low-income families is affected much more by changes in deductions and exemptions than by changes in marginal tax rates. As a result, the amount of tax relief for those at the bottom was minimal. The effective federal income tax rate on the poorest 20 percent of families increased from 8.1 to 10.4 percent between 1980 and 1985, while it declined from 29.7 to 24.4 percent for the richest 5 percent of families (U.S. House of Representatives, 1993). The average federal tax bill for a family with income at the poverty line increased from 4.0 percent of income in 1978 to 10.4 percent in 1986.[4]

In addition to these tax changes, changes in social welfare programs also hurt the poor. The Omnibus Budget Reconciliation Act (OBRA) of 1981 substantially reduced spending on programs for children. While inflation had eroded nominal benefit levels during the Carter administration, OBRA signaled the first direct retrenchments in programs. Particularly hard hit were the Comprehensive Employment and Training Act (CETA), Unemployment Insurance (UI), and Aid to Families with Dependent Children (AFDC). Congress eliminated the CETA program entirely and replaced it with the smaller Job Training Partnership Act (JTPA).

At its peak, CETA had funded more than three-quarters of a million full-time public service jobs. JTPA funds training, but not wages, for a smaller number of participants, who are enrolled, on average, for less than half the year. Spending on employment and training programs fell from about $22 billion to about $8 billion (in 1992 dollars) between 1979 and 1982. To put this reduction in context, total spending for the Food Stamp program in 1982 was about $16 billion (in 1992 dollars).[5] Spending was also reduced for Food Stamps, school lunches, legal services, and social services.

In addition, real spending for unemployment compensation fell by more than 25 percent between 1980 and 1985. During the 1974–1975 recession, Congress had extended unemployment insurance several times, so that in 1975 almost three-quarters of the unemployed received UI benefits. For most of the period between 1950 and 1980 about half of the unemployed received benefits, but by the mid-1980s, because of program changes implemented by OBRA, only about one-third did so. These changes in employment programs and unemployment compensation meant that workers in the turbulent labor market of the 1980s were more economically vulnerable and had less assistance to retrain and prepare for another job than had been the case a decade earlier.

The changes in AFDC contained in OBRA provide a good example of the philosophical shift in antipoverty policy under the Reagan presidency (see Glazer, 1984). The administration argued that eligibility for welfare benefits had increased so much in some states because many who were not "truly needy" remained on the welfare rolls. Work effort, according to this view, was best promoted by work requirements (proposed by the President, but not enacted), not by work incentives. Welfare should not encourage simultaneous receipt of wages and welfare benefits; it should be a safety net, providing cash assistance only for those unable to secure jobs. For example, in 1980 forty-two states, but by 1984 only seven states, would provide some AFDC benefits to a woman with two children who had earnings at 75 percent of her poverty line (U.S. House of Representatives, 1993, p. 1242).

Several changes in benefit calculations and eligibility criteria resulted in reductions in AFDC. Among the most influential was the elimination of the "30 and a third rule," which allowed beneficiaries to make $30 per month before losing any benefits and then reduced benefits by $2 for every $3 earned. Under OBRA, after a recipient had been on the rolls for four months, benefits were reduced by a dollar for every dollar earned. OBRA also instituted maximum limits above which a state could not pay benefits. By early 1983, 490,000 working families, nearly 14 percent of all beneficiaries, had been removed from the AFDC rolls. Poor families affected by these cuts lost between $1,300 and $2,500 in annual income (U.S. General Accounting Office, 1984; Primus, 1989). The President justified these cuts as necessary to control federal spending and as a way to offset the tax revenues lost due to the income tax reductions. This rationalization was less important than the signal it sent about changing the nature of welfare programs, because the savings to government were relatively small.

To make matters worse, these cuts in social welfare spending took effect just as the economy soured. The recession that began in July 1981 and ended in November 1982 was particularly severe. The unemployment rate exceeded 10 percent for the first time since the Great Depression. With decreased government assistance, families with children were particularly vulnerable. The child poverty rate increased from 16.4 percent to 20 percent between 1979 and 1981 because of the earlier recession and the high inflation rate. It then increased further to 22.3 percent in 1983.

The contrast between the Reagan retrenchment and the benefit expansion of the War on Poverty–Great Society era is striking. Spending on federal social programs grew very rapidly through the mid-1970s. The average annual real growth rates of federal social spending were 7.9 percent during the Kennedy-Johnson years and 9.7 percent during the Nixon-Ford years (Palmer and Sawhill, 1984,

p. 350). By the late 1970s real growth in benefits slowed, primarily because many benefits were not indexed for inflation. Real federal social welfare spending grew by less than 4 percent per year during the Carter presidency, and only one program to aid low-income people, the Low Income Energy Assistance program, was established. During the first Reagan administration, the real growth rate of social programs fell to about 1.5 percent per year, and major structural changes designed to reduce most programs (except Social Security retirement benefits and some benefits for the disabled) were undertaken. If Social Security, Medicare, Medicaid, and other health expenditures are excluded, federal spending for social welfare programs declined by about 3 percent between fiscal years 1981 and 1985 (Falk, Nuschler, and Rimkunas, 1993).

Despite the Reagan retrenchment, total federal social spending in the mid-1990s remained well above the pre-1965 level, primarily because of continuing increases in health and Social Security spending (Burtless, 1994). The expansion of social welfare programs was halted, but most programs (except CETA) were still in place.

Social spending by state governments was also restricted in the early 1980s. While a few states changed welfare benefits and regulations to offset some of the negative impact of OBRA, most accepted the retrenchment. Others even compounded them by reducing state AFDC benefits. This reinforcement of the Reagan retrenchment was due to both the increasing conservatism of state governments and the decreases in state revenue caused by the 1981–1982 recession.

President Reagan accomplished a major reorientation in public policies. Congress enacted a large tax cut, authorized a five-year, trillion-dollar defense buildup, and restricted social welfare spending. These changes, according to the administration's projections, would stimulate economic growth and lead to a balanced federal budget. When this did not happen, concern about the resulting deficits, along with the administration's pessimistic view about the ability of government to deal with social problems, meant that spending for domestic programs generally, and antipoverty programs particularly, would bear the brunt of attempts to control spending and reduce the deficit (see Peterson, 1985). Social programs lost quickly and decisively to the politics of defense and deficits.

The 1980s also ushered in the longest period of divided government in the history of the nation. As a result, even though the Reagan administration continued to propose further reductions in anti-poverty programs, Congress balked. The effects of the 1981 program reductions, the increased poverty and economic hardship brought about by the 1981–1982 recession, and the increasing attention paid to the medically uninsured and the homeless kept Congress from continuing the budgetary retrenchment.

The administration's reliance on economic growth as its only anti-poverty strategy was a catalyst for congressional opposition. The House Ways and Means Committee documented that almost half a million people had become poor as a result of the OBRA 1981 policies (U.S. House of Representatives, 1984) and began to advocate expansion of social welfare programs. Divided government and continuing deficits, however, prevented the enactment of major legislation to deal with poverty. A lack of organized lobbying on behalf of the poor also contributed to this failure to act (Primus, 1989; Weaver, 1985), as did the fact that antipoverty programs remained politically unpopular.

Congress did reverse some aspects of the retrenchment by providing modest increases in funding and restoring some program provisions. For example, AFDC rules and Food Stamp funding were liberalized somewhat in 1984, and Medicaid was revised several times to increase coverage of poor children. Not until the Family Support Act of 1988, however, would major legislation targeted on a social welfare program pass Congress and be signed into law.

A New Social Policy Consensus

The Reagan administration's main social policy was an emphasis on the primary importance of a growing economy. In its 1982 *Economic Report of the President*, the Council of Economic Advisers defended the administration's budget cuts on the grounds that they would stimulate economic growth that would eventually benefit the poor: "Many of the Administration's policies have reduced government expenditures for various groups or provided less of an increase in such outlays than has been expected. The fundamental premise behind these reductions is that they ultimately will lead to substantial and sustainable economic growth. This has particular relevance for the poor, most of whom probably have historically benefited more from sustained economic growth than from government transfer programs" (p. 44).

While President Johnson's advisers had advocated growth plus an activist policy, Reagan's advisers relied on growth alone. They expected the poverty rate to fall as the economy recovered from the 1981–1982 recession. The economy did expand for more than seven years, exceeding administration expectations, but as we will document in the next chapter, poverty declined only slightly and inequality increased.

Most of the increased economic hardship of the 1980s was due to technological changes, the globalization of markets, and other structural changes in the labor market that increased the demand for higher-skilled relative to lower-skilled workers. Younger workers, blue-collar workers, and workers with less than a college degree have all fared badly in the labor market over the last two decades, particularly since the late 1970s. (We discuss these changes in detail in Chapters 6 and 7.)

What matters here is that government tax and transfer policies would have had to become more redistributive than they had been in the 1970s just to keep poverty and inequality constant. Instead, because of the Reagan philosophy and legislative changes, income tax and antipoverty policies became less progressive.

Simply put, throughout the 1980s economic growth did little to help poor and low-income workers, and government policies were not reoriented to counter these adverse changes in the labor market. Social programs lifted fewer families, especially families with children, out of poverty in the 1980s than in the 1970s for two reasons. First, the percentage of the working poor served by the programs declined after Reagan's initial budget reductions. Second, real benefits continued to decline, as nominal benefit levels in many programs did not keep pace with the modest inflation of the 1980s.

The continuing economic hardship for many families focused attention on the growing gaps between the rich and the poor and the rich and the middle class. As a result, Congress and the public became much more skeptical about the view that the benefits of a growing economy would "trickle down" to the poor. In the mid-1980s, Congress and the President had begun negotiations to reform the federal tax system. This provided an opportunity to move away from "trickle-down" economics. Reducing the income tax burden on working poor families became a key goal for tax reform.

The Tax Reform Act of 1986

Because the 1981 tax act had not increased the standard deduction or the personal exemption, the tax burden for the working poor increased while the burden on higher-income groups became lighter. As the debate regarding tax reform progressed, both Republicans and Democrats agreed to aid low-income families. President Reagan favored any opportunity to reduce taxes; Democrats saw such tax relief as a way to raise the living standards of low-income families and to achieve greater equity. In its final form, the Tax Reform Act of 1986 restored some progressivity to the tax code, especially for low-income wage earners. For persons earning less than $10,000, effective tax rates dropped from 1.6 to 0.5 percent of income; for families with incomes between $10,000 and $20,000, effective rates dropped from 7.5 to 5.7 percent (Steuerle, 1991, p. 122). While these reductions did not raise disposable income by very much, they did provide the first direct increase in government assistance to low-income families since the late 1970s.

The Tax Reform Act was particularly beneficial to working poor families with children, because it expanded the Earned Income Tax Credit (EITC). The EITC, enacted in 1975, provides families of the working poor with a refundable income tax credit; that is, the family receives a payment if the credit due exceeds the income tax owed.[6] The EITC raises the effective wage of low-income families. It is available to both one- and two-parent families and does not require them to apply for welfare. The maximum EITC for a poor family was $400 in 1975 and rose only to $550 by 1986.

In 1986 the expansion of the EITC received broad bipartisan support. The Act gradually increased the EITC so that by 1990 a working parent received an additional fourteen cents for every dollar earned up to $6,807, where the credit reached its maximum value of $953. The EITC then remained at $953 until earned income rose to $10,740, after which it was phased out at a rate of ten cents per dollar earned above that level. The 1986 Act significantly increased the number of families receiving credits. Between 5 and 7.5 million families a year received credits between 1975 and 1986. In 1988 this number rose to more than 11 million. As a result, the federal income and payroll tax burden on a family of four with income at the poverty line fell from 10.4 percent in 1986 to 2.5 percent in 1990. (The EITC was expanded again in 1990 and 1993.)

In addition to offsetting Social Security taxes and increasing the disposable income of working poor families with children, the EITC provides encouragement to work. For example, if someone is offered the 1994 minimum wage of $4.25, but also receives an EITC of 30 percent, then the effective wage is just above $5.50.[7] If the employer is not willing to pay this worker more than $4.25, but the worker is unwilling to accept any job paying less than $5.50 per hour, the EITC bridges this gap and leads the worker to accept the minimum-wage job. The dual functions of the EITC as income support and work incentive contributed to its bipartisan popularity.

The Family Support Act of 1988

In addition to tax reform, Congress, after protracted discussions, passed the Family Support Act (FSA) of 1988. This Act represents another example of the shift away from the Reagan retrenchment toward a bipartisan social policy consensus. During the congressional debate, more liberal welfare reform provisions proposed by House Democrats and more conservative provisions proposed by Senate Republicans and supported by the Reagan administration were both rejected. The FSA promoted the new consensus by requiring custodial and absent parents to take more responsibility for supporting their children who receive welfare. Custodial parents are expected to work more, absent parents to pay more child support.

The FSA extended eligibility for welfare by requiring all states to provide AFDC for at least six months each year to two-parent families in which the primary earner is unemployed. Before 1988 only about half of the states provided any welfare benefits to such families. FSA also strengthened the enforcement of child support requirements. States were required to establish and update child-support guidelines, make a greater effort to establish paternity for children born out of wedlock (Social Security numbers of both parents are now required in most cases before a state issues a birth certificate), and automatically withhold child-support payments from the earnings of absent parents.

Most important, the FSA established a new work, training, and education program for AFDC recipients—the Job Opportunities and Basic Skills Training Program (JOBS). JOBS became a central feature of the FSA in part because of the success of many state "workfare" demonstration programs that were undertaken in response to OBRA 1981. The Manpower Demonstration Research Corporation (MDRC) evaluated state programs during the 1980s and found many of them modestly successful in reducing dependence on welfare and increasing earnings. More important for liberals, who tended to oppose workfare, was the finding that many participants judged the programs fair and helpful in connecting them to the work force. The evaluations were promising enough that, by the late 1980s, moving welfare recipients into employment had become a bipartisan aspect of the new consensus.[8]

Liberals and conservatives still disagreed on the other goals of welfare-to-work programs. Liberals viewed welfare reform as offering opportunities for welfare mothers to receive training and work experience that would help them raise their families' living standards by working more and at higher wages. Conservatives emphasized work requirements, obligations welfare mothers owed in return for government support whether or not their families' incomes increased.

The MDRC evaluations produced some results that satisfied both groups. In their comprehensive review, Gueron and Pauly (1991) found that successful programs modestly reduced welfare dependence and encouraged some recipients to leave the welfare rolls. The early state programs primarily consisted of employment counseling and assistance in searching for jobs. By the end of the 1980s programs also provided recipients with such services as subsidized child care and transportation, follow-up counseling after employment began, and education and training services.

The typical welfare participant who received training, education, or job placement earned about 15–30 percent more during the first two years than the typical member of the control group of recipients who did not participate in the program. While these were substantial percentage gains, monthly earnings in the second year remained below $200 per month on average and most participants remained poor. Employment rates for participants and controls were about 34 and 30 percent, respectively, after two years. AFDC participation and state welfare spending also declined modestly. After three years, 39.2 percent of the participants and 42.6 percent of controls remained on AFDC.

The JOBS component of FSA incorporated many of the lessons of the MDRC demonstrations. States were required to implement welfare-to-work programs and extend them to a greater proportion of their caseload. However, they were allowed great latitude in shaping their own programs, and the startup period was a long one. By 1995 only 20 percent of the caseload was required to participate in such programs. States also had to offer a broad range of education, skills training, job placement, and support services for such items as child care and transportation.

The FSA was a major welfare reform, but its accomplishments should be placed in context. To date, the Act has been more important for its contribution to the new consensus than for its impact on welfare recipients. The FSA, building on a fifty-year tradition of shared governmental responsibility for AFDC, assigned to state governments the primary responsibility for reforming welfare programs and ending long-term welfare dependency. Unfortunately, however, the FSA took effect just as the economic expansion of the 1980s ended. State governments faced falling revenues and increasing costs for current services, and few were inclined to begin major new social initiatives. Thus states tended to avoid programs that required increased expenditures in the initial years, even innovative ones that promised to save more money in future years.[9]

Nonworking welfare recipients now receive substantially lower benefits than did similar recipients two decades ago. Figure 2.1 presents the combined AFDC and Food Stamp benefits, in constant

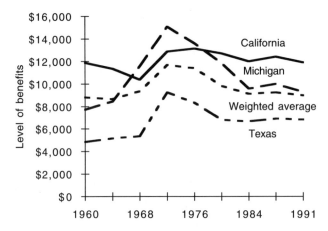

Figure 2.1 Combined AFDC and Food Stamp benefits (family of four with no other income), 1960–1991. Weighted average: mean of each state weighted by number of recipients per state (Michigan figures for Wayne County). Figures in 1991 dollars. (Source: *Green Book*, various years.)

1991 dollars, for the past thirty years, for a family of four with no other income in three states, along with the weighted average (by number of recipients) for all states. (Michigan and California are typical of high-benefit states; Texas, of low-benefit states.) In 1960 in Michigan, for example, a family of this type would have received about $7,700 from AFDC. By 1972, with the addition of Food Stamps, benefits increased to about $15,000, which was above the $13,812 poverty line for such a family. Since that time welfare benefits have been eroded by inflation (especially from the mid-1970s to early 1980s), by program restrictions in the early 1980s, and by reductions in nominal benefit levels in a number of states in the early 1990s. By 1991 combined benefits had fallen to $9,260, or about two-thirds of the poverty line. Benefits in Michigan were 39 percent lower in 1991 than in 1972. For the median state, the maximum AFDC benefit alone declined by more than 40 percent between 1972 and 1991, while the maximum for AFDC plus Food Stamps declined by 23 percent.

These data suggest that poverty rates remain high because we have cut back so much on direct cash assistance and have done so little to improve welfare recipients' employment opportunities and prospects for obtaining child support. The early experience with the FSA suggests that reducing poverty rates will require a substantial financial commitment from the federal and state governments. More must be done to help welfare recipients enter the labor market and achieve economic self-sufficiency.

The 1990 Budget Summit

The Budget Act of 1990 is primarily remembered for President Bush's decision to raise taxes, breaking his pledge not to do so. The motivation behind the Act was to reduce the deficit. As a result, taxes were raised overall. They were reduced for the working poor, however, through another substantial expansion of the EITC. The maximum benefit and the subsidy rate in the EITC were again increased, and the thresholds determining the benefit levels were indexed for inflation for the years after 1992. Also, a higher EITC was established for families with more than one child. The maximum credit was increased from $953 in 1990 to $2,008 in 1994. As a result, the federal income and payroll tax burden on a family of four at the poverty line fell from 2.5 percent in 1990 to −2.1 percent (a refund) in 1994.[10]

In response to the 1990–1991 recession, President Bush and Congress also extended the length of time over which unemployment insurance benefits could be received. And in 1990, after prolonged negotiations, the President signed into law the first increase in the minimum wage since the Carter administration. While it was not large enough to compensate for the erosion in the minimum wage due to inflation since the previous increase, it did amount to nearly a 30 percent increase (in two steps) from $3.35 per hour to $4.25 per hour.[11]

The Clinton Antipoverty Policies

These changes in tax and transfer policy in the late 1980s partially offset the negative effects on the poor of changes made during the early years of the Reagan presidency. Although they did not amount to a major new antipoverty initiative, they did represent another shift in policy priorities. In retrospect, the official perspective on antipoverty policy was overly optimistic when the War on Poverty was declared and overly pessimistic when the Reagan administration began to shrink the social safety net. The experience of the 1980s provided a "pseudo-social experiment" for evaluating whether policies designed to promote economic growth were sufficient to reduce poverty. Average living standards did increase, but the poor gained little during this period of modest growth.

The continuing economic hardship pushed Congress and the public away from the view that economic growth alone could solve the plight of the poor. President Bush was perceived as inattentive to the problems of the poor and the unemployed during the 1990–1991 recession. This perception contributed to the election of President Clinton, who, during the campaign, emphasized the new consensus that supplementing the earnings of low-wage workers should be a top priority of antipoverty policy and that benefits for recipients able to work but not doing so should not be increased: "It's time to honor and reward people who work hard and play by the rules. That means ending welfare as we know it—not by punishing the poor or preaching to them, but by empowering Americans to take care of their children and improve their lives. No one who works full time and has children at home should be poor anymore. No one who can work should be able to stay on welfare forever" (Clinton, 1992).

More was to be done for the poor, but more was to be expected of them as well. This determination to fight poverty by supplementing low wages differs significantly from the consensus of the 1970s that cash welfare benefits should be universally available (for example, President Nixon's Family Assistance Plan and President Carter's Program for Better Jobs and Income).[12] This new consensus builds on the JOBS component of the Family Support Act and was a key feature of President Clinton's 1994 welfare reform proposal. That proposal was set aside, however, when the Republicans gained control of Congress. It would have placed a two-year time limit on welfare benefits. Recipients who had not found a private-sector job after reaching the time limit would have been offered positions in public jobs programs (Lehman and Danziger, 1995). Republicans endorsed the concept of a time limit but rejected spending on public employ-ment and sought to reduce the size and scope of existing programs.

The President proposed and Congress did pass another major ex-pansion of the Earned Income Tax Credit in 1993. By 1998 the EITC will provide almost $25 billion to working-poor and low-income families, more than total AFDC spending, and an increase of about $7 billion per year beyond what the earlier law would have pro-vided. In 1994 President Clinton proposed, but Congress rejected, universal coverage for medical care, another key feature designed to "make work pay" for low-income workers. The Clinton administra-tion also unsuccessfully proposed legislation to reorient education, employment, and training programs.

At first it seemed that the Clinton administration would bring about another major shift in antipoverty policy. Its agenda to "make work pay" and "end welfare as we know it" reflected the political and policy lessons of the past three decades. It occupied a middle ground between the optimism about government's ability to re-solve social problems that characterized the War on Poverty and the pessimism of the Reagan era. And it seemed to have broad biparti-san support when it reemphasized one of the goals of the War on Poverty—that the way to fight poverty is to offer a hand up and not a handout for those who are able to work. It rejected both the asser-tions that government can do almost anything and that government can do almost nothing.

The only victory in antipoverty policy of the first two years of the Clinton administration, however, was the expansion of the EITC. The conservative Republican majority that took over both houses of Congress in 1995 immediately set aside Clinton's agenda for do-mestic reform. The Republicans made cutting government spending in general, and social welfare spending in particular, a top priority in their "Contract with America."

Whereas the Clinton administration represented a middle ground in antipoverty policy, the Republicans have returned to the bud-getary retrenchment and "government is the problem" view of the Reagan administration. It is too early to know how successful they will be in cutting social spending. But our analysis in the next two chapters demonstrates that cuts in social programs of the magnitude proposed in the Contract with America would increase poverty and economic hardship.

In Chapter 8 we will propose several antipoverty reforms consistent with the consensus that developed in the 1980s, even though that consensus now seems to have been set aside. We reject the assertions that reductions in spending on the poor can promote self-sufficiency and that spending for the most vulnerable should be cut to pay for tax cuts for the middle and upper classes. We set out an alternative approach that requires increased spending in the short run to foster self-sufficiency and to reduce poverty in the long run. We show that carefully designed government policies can make a difference. We are realistic enough to recognize that policies that are politically and economically feasible in the mid-1990s will not totally eliminate poverty, but we are confident enough to argue that the money would be well spent.

Chapter 3

Trends in the Level and Distribution of Income

The conventional wisdom about the relationships between economic growth and poverty and between economic growth and income inequality has changed radically since the early 1980s. Jeffrey Williamson and Peter Lindert (1980), using a model that had successfully depicted two centuries of inequality in the United States, projected falling inequality for the 1980s. Peter Gottschalk (1981) was similarly optimistic about the trend in poverty, predicting a poverty rate for 1985 that turned out to be substantially lower than the actual rate for that year. These and other researchers did not foresee the slowdown in the growth of average earnings, the rise in earnings inequality, the continuing high rates of poverty, or the diminished governmental concern with poverty and inequality that characterized the 1980s.

In an important review article in 1980, Alan Blinder concluded: "The more things change, the more they remain the same . . . when we consider the distribution of economic welfare—economic equality, as it is commonly called—the central stylized fact is one of constancy. As measured in the official data, income inequality was just about the same in 1977 . . . as it was in 1947" (1980, p. 416). Fourteen years later, when Blinder was a member of President Clinton's Council of Economic Advisers, the situation had changed. In the 1994 *Economic Report of the President*, he and his colleagues called attention to increasing inequality: "In the last two decades, family income growth has stagnated and incomes have become more unequally distributed. In fact, the real incomes of the bottom 60 percent of American families were lower in the early 1990s than for the analogous families at the end of the 1970s" (p. 14).

We now review the economic experience that has led to this dramatic shift in the conventional wisdom. We begin by examining the broad trends in the published data on median and mean family income, family income inequality, and the official poverty rate, and by reviewing the criticisms that have been levied against the published data. We then present our own time series on trends in the level and distribution of income after 1949. Our series differ in several important respects from the published ones, because we have incorporated several modifications into our measures that respond to these criticisms. For details about the published data and our tabulations based on unpublished Census data, see "A Note on the Data," page 177.

The Level of Family Income

Figure 3.1 and columns 1 and 2 of Table 3.1 show the trends in median and mean family income from 1947 through 1991. The published Census data in the table are expressed in constant 1990 dollars, adjusted for inflation using the consumer price index (CPI-U) from 1947 to 1983 and the CPI-U-X1 from 1983 to 1991.[1]

Median family income is the most common measure of the nation's standard of living. It reveals how the "typical" American is faring, as half of all families are doing worse and half are doing better than the median family. The median is less affected by changes at the upper and lower ends of the distribution than is the mean. For example, if the incomes of most families rise slightly but those of a small number of the richest families rise sharply, the mean will rise more than the median.

As long as growth is relatively constant across the entire range of incomes, as it was for the three decades after World War II, trends in median and mean family income will be similar. But if the incomes of the rich are growing much more rapidly than those of average families, as was the case in the 1980s, the mean will increase more

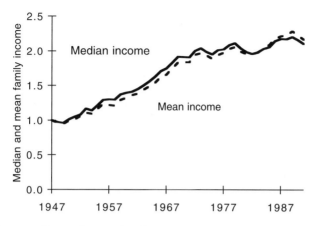

Figure 3.1 Median and mean family income, 1947–1991. Indexed at 1.00 in 1947. (Source: U.S. Bureau of the Census, Current Population Reports, ser. P-60.)

rapidly than the median. Note in Figure 3.1 that the median grew slightly faster than the mean from 1947 until 1980. After that point, the mean grew faster than the median, an indication that inequality was increasing.[2]

Both median and mean family income grew almost continuously from 1949 through 1973. During that twenty-five-year period, year-to-year changes in median income were positive twenty times and negative only four times. The largest decline was about 1.3 percent during the 1969–1971 recession. The median increased by 43 percent between 1949 and 1959, and by another 39 percent between 1959 and 1969. The mean increased a little less in the first decade, 37 percent, and by about the same amount in the next, 42 percent. Both median and mean family income doubled between 1949 and 1973.

If any period can be called the "good old days," 1949–1973 was it with respect to family income. In fact, the postwar boom was so robust that its continuation was taken for granted when the War on Poverty was declared. In the 1967 *Economic Report of the President* the Council of Economic Advisers noted: "The United States is the first large nation in the history of the world wealthy enough to end

Table 3.1   The level and distribution of family income, selected years, 1947–1991 (1990 dollars)[a]

Year	Median income	Mean income	Percentage distribution of aggregate income					
			Lowest quintile	Second quintile	Third quintile	Fourth quintile	Highest quintile	Top 5 percent
1947	$16,345	$19,123	5.0	11.9	17.0	23.1	43.0	17.5
1949	$15,699	$18,034	4.5	11.9	17.3	23.5	42.7	16.9
1954	$18,629	$20,940	4.5	12.1	17.7	23.9	41.8	16.3
1959	$22,386	$24,696	4.9	12.3	17.9	23.8	41.1	15.9
1964	$25,483	$28,459	5.1	12.0	17.7	24.0	41.2	15.9
1969	$31,292	$35,087	5.6	12.4	17.7	23.7	40.6	15.6
1974	$32,490	$37,047	5.5	12.0	17.5	24.0	41.0	15.5
1979	$34,595	$39,415	5.2	11.6	17.5	24.1	41.7	15.8
1984	$33,251	$39,062	4.7	11.0	17.0	24.4	42.9	16.0
1989	$36,062	$43,749	4.6	10.6	16.5	23.7	44.6	17.9
1991	$34,488	$41,491	4.5	10.7	16.6	24.1	44.2	17.1

Source: U.S. Bureau of the Census, Current Population Reports, ser. P-60. This table contains information on selected years; data from every year in the Census Bureau publications are used in Figures 3.1, 3.4, and 3.7.

a. Inflation is measured by the CPI-U (price index for urban consumers) from 1947 to 1967, and by the CPI-U-X1 from 1968 onward.

poverty within its borders" (p. 16). Conventional wisdom held not only that the United States was much richer than it had been two decades earlier but also that it was richer than any other country.

Neither of these conditions holds true today. The oil shock of 1973 plus slower growth in productivity brought an end to this remarkable quarter-century of rising living standards, and to the optimistic view that American incomes would continue to grow and would always exceed those of other countries. Our economic history since 1973 differs markedly. Even a casual inspection of Figure 3.1 shows that income growth became erratic. Since 1973 the median income has shown about as many year-to-year declines as increases.

The recession that began in November 1973 was the longest and steepest since the late 1930s, lasting sixteen months.[3] The recovery started in March 1975, and mean family income nearly regained its

1973 level by the end of 1979. However, the economy again slid into recession at the beginning of 1980. While this downturn lasted only six months, the subsequent recovery was also brief, lasting only a year. The economy then went into a long and steep recession which extended until November 1982. By that time median family income was 7.4 percent below its 1979 value and 4 percent below its 1973 value. This poor economic performance is what led Frank Levy to label this decade the "quiet depression." For the first time since the Great Depression, the "typical" family was worse off than its counterpart had been a decade earlier.

Starting from this low base in November 1982, the economy entered a long and relatively strong recovery that lasted until July 1990: the second-longest recovery on record. While mean and median family income grew fairly rapidly during the recovery, the growth was not nearly as fast as that in the 1960s.[4] On the other hand, it was stellar compared with that of the 1970s. By 1989 median family income finally exceeded that of 1979, the previous peak, by 4.2 percent. Thus, while the growth was not unprecedented, the length and strength of the recovery led to average incomes in 1989 that were higher than ever before.

The paradox we address in this book is the coincidence of higher poverty and higher inequality with these all-time-high average incomes. Why didn't the poverty rate fall as rapidly during the economic expansion of the 1980s as it did during that of the 1960s? If economic growth is the main engine driving down the poverty rate, then the poverty rate should have been at an all-time low in 1989. Not only was it still relatively high, but it was at a level first reached in 1968, twenty-one years earlier. To put it another way, the 8 percent increase in median family income between 1973 and 1989 had no effect on the proportion of the population with incomes below the official poverty line.

Median income fell by 4.4 percent between 1989 and 1991 because of recession. The net result was that the 1970s and 1980s produced almost no improvement in the median standard of living.

One possible response to these facts, which are based on an analysis of the published data, is that the measure of family income is flawed. Some researchers have argued that the official measure understates both the rate of income growth and the reduction in poverty because it does not take into account noncash benefits such as food stamps. Others argue that demographic changes, particularly the shift toward female-headed families, explain the paradox. We will consider several criticisms of the published measures and describe our adjustments to the data to correct the flaws in the official measures. After the adjustments, however, as we will show, the paradox of rising median income and a continuing high poverty rate remains. No matter how measured, income growth and the decline in poverty were much slower in the two decades after 1973 than in the previous two decades.

Adjustments to the Measure of Family Income

Several flaws can be noted in the data used to measure trends in family income. First, the published series on family incomes do not take into account a substantial and rapidly increasing portion of our population—unrelated individuals. Second, they do not take into account the decline in average family size.

The Census Bureau publishes a time series on mean per capita income that does include unrelated individuals and does incorporate an adjustment for family size. In the family income series, however, all families with the same income are considered economically equivalent, regardless of the size of their families. For example, if a family of three and a family of six both report annual incomes of $30,000, the two families are considered to be equally well-off. This is equivalent to assuming that increases in family size do not increase a family's expenses—but while rent and car payments may not change, expenses for food certainly do increase. Measuring family income without adjusting for family size implies that two can live as cheaply as one, or that economies of scale are very large.

Measures of per capita income reflect another extreme assumption: the opposite one, that each family member consumes an equal share of the family's resources. Thus, in the example above, in which each family has an annual income of $30,000, the family with three members has a per capita income that is twice that of the family of six. This measure also implies that all persons require the same resources whether they live alone or in families. In other words, there are no economies of scale, and two need exactly twice as much as one to maintain their standard of living.

We believe neither of these two extremes is the appropriate way to adjust income for family size. In our analyses we incorporate a different adjustment. The "equivalence scale" we use to compare family incomes is derived from the official poverty lines and reflects modest economies of scale. That is, a larger family needs a larger income to be as well-off as a smaller family, but that need does not increase by the same amount as each additional person is added to the household. For example, the poverty line for a two-person family is about two-thirds that for a four-person family, implying that a four-person family needs about one and one-half times as much income as a two-person family. We use the same equivalence scale as that used in determining the official poverty line and therefore consider a two-person family with an income of $10,000 as well-off as a four-person family with an income of $15,000.

Some adjustment for family size is clearly needed, as family size has declined dramatically over the past four decades and the number of unrelated individuals has increased much faster than the number of families. In other words, the number of income-sharing units has grown faster than the population, and the typical family has gotten smaller.[5]

We adjust the Census and CPS microeconomic data by including unrelated individuals, using the equivalence scale implicit in the official poverty lines, and by applying the procedures incorporated in the post-1983 price index for the entire period after 1967. We also weight our adjusted income measure by the number of persons in each family to take account of the fact that more persons are affected by changes in incomes in large families than in small families. The official poverty measure is based on these same procedures: it includes all families and unrelated individuals, it counts each person once, and it adjusts for family size differences using this equivalence scale. The major difference between our poverty measures and the official time series is that we incorporate the revised price index known as the CPI-U-X1 beginning in 1968, while the Census incorporates it in 1983; see "A Note on the Data," page 177.

Our measures of poverty and median income are based on a consistent concept of income; those of the Census are not.

Table 3.2 contrasts our measure of living standards—median adjusted income of persons divided by the poverty line—with the Census Bureau's median family income for selected years from 1949 to 1991.[6] According to our measure, the median person in 1991 lived in a family whose income was 3.14 times the poverty line.

The official poverty line is adjusted for inflation. As a result, any differences in this measure from year to year represent real dif-

Table 3.2   Trends in median family income and median adjusted income, divided by the poverty line, selected years, 1949–1991

	Real median family income[a]	Real median adjusted income for all persons[b]
1949	$15,699	1.24
1959	$22,386	1.86
1969	$31,292	2.51
% change 1949–1969	99.3%	102.4%
1973	$33,370	2.84
1979	$34,595	3.05
1982	$32,037	2.87
1989	$36,062	3.31
1991	$34,488	3.14
% change 1973–1991	3.4%	10.6%

Source: Authors' calculations from computer tapes of Decennial Censuses of Population and March Current Population Surveys.

a. Column 1 is in 1990 constant dollars. The published data on median family income exclude unrelated individuals, make no adjustment for family size, and count each family once.

b. Our adjustment uses the Census microdata for 1949 to 1969 and the CPS microdata from 1973 to the present. We include unrelated individuals as one-person families, divide family income by the poverty line to adjust for family-size differences, and weight each family by the total number of its members. Because the poverty line is adjusted for inflation, our measure of median-adjusted income corrects for inflation when we divide income by the poverty line. The value 3.14 for 1991 reflects the fact that the median individual lived in a family that had income a little more than three times the poverty line.

ferences in income. For example, the CPI-U-X1 poverty line for a family of four was $4,437 in 1973 and $12,667 in 1991. If the income of a family of four increased from $4,437 to $15,200 between 1973 and 1991, our measure would reflect this as a real increase in adjusted income of 20 percent, from 1.0 to 1.2 times the poverty line.

Our measure grows a bit faster than the published measure during the two long periods highlighted in Table 3.2, but the major trends are the same. Family incomes doubled between 1949 and 1969 but increased only slightly from 1973 to 1991. Between 1949 and 1969 the median family income increased from $15,699 to $31,292; the typical American lived in a family with income 24 percent above the poverty line in 1949, and about 2.5 times the poverty line in 1969.

For the period 1973–1991, income divided by the poverty line grew by 10.6 percent while the median family income grew by only 3.4 percent. Our measure suggests that the median standard of living grew by 15.3 percent during the 1982–1989 recovery, whereas the published median increased by 12.6 percent.

Although income grew very slowly after 1973, the typical American's standard of living reached an all-time high in 1989. This, of course, does not mean that everyone was better off, only that after considering gainers and losers there was higher income in the aggregate at the end of the 1980s than at the beginning.

Our next task is to examine how those at the bottom and at the top of the distribution fared and how the changes in their incomes compared with those of the rest of the population. We will examine both inequality in incomes and poverty. Poverty, as measured in the United States, focuses on the *absolute* living standards of those with the least resources; income inequality focuses on how far the living standards of those at the bottom and the top deviate from those at the median.[7]

Income Inequality

In order to document the trend in inequality of family incomes, we review the time series for two summary measures from the published Current Population Surveys (CPS) for the period 1947–1991. We then return to our measure of adjusted income divided by the poverty line for our analysis of inequality.

The first summary measure is the ratio of the real income of a family at the 80th percentile (80 percent of the families have a lower income than this family) to that of a family at the 20th percentile (20 percent of families have a lower income). Figure 3.2 charts this ratio from 1947 to 1991. For example, the value of 3.71 in 1991 indicates that the family at the 80th percentile received an income ($62,991), almost four times as large as that of the family at the 20th percentile ($17,000).

As the figure shows, this measure fluctuated in a rather narrow band between 1947 and 1969. Changes in inequality were dominated by cyclical fluctuations. The ratio was highest, at about 3.3, in 1949, 1954, 1961 (ends of three recessions), and 1963. As the economy boomed during the 1960s, the income gap between families at the bottom and those near the top narrowed and the ratio fell below 3.0.

Viewed from the perspective of the 1990s, the origins of today's large gap between those at the top and those at the bottom can be

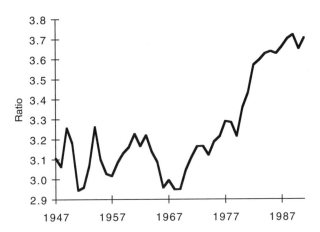

Figure 3.2   Ratio: income of family at 80th percentile to that of family at 20th percentile, 1947–1991. (Source: U.S. Bureau of the Census, Current Population Reports, ser. P-60.)

found after the 1969–1970 recession. From that year forward, the gap has increased during both recessions and recoveries, with the most rapid increase coming between 1979 and 1989, when the ratio increased from 3.22 to 3.72. From the perspective of the early 1980s, however, it is easy to understand why the conventional wisdom held that during the postwar boom a rising tide lifted all boats. Economic growth had been rapid and had benefited families at the 20th as well as at the 80th percentile. The ratio of the income of the 80th percentile to that at the 20th was virtually the same in 1979 (3.22) as in 1949 (3.26).

Figure 3.3 presents annual data on mean (inflation-adjusted) family income, the income of the 80th percentile (lower limit of top quintile), and that of the 20th percentile (upper limit of bottom quintile). These data represent in 1991 dollars what was emphasized in Figures 3.1 and 3.2—that rapid growth in the mean in the early period was evenly shared, and that slow growth in the later period did not trickle down to the poor.

Between 1947 and 1969 the income of a family at the 20th percentile just about doubled (from $8,915 to $17,284). But the income of a family at the 20th percentile was actually lower in 1991

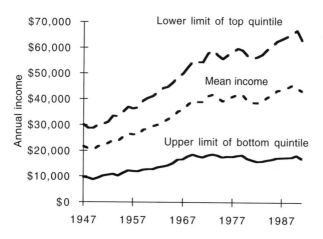

Figure 3.3 Family income at three points in the income distribution, 1947–1991. Figures in 1991 dollars. (Source: U.S. Bureau of the Census, Current Population Reports, ser. P-60.)

($17,000) than in 1969. The ratio of the 80th to the 20th percentile increased over this period, because although income was stagnant at the bottom of the distribution, income at the 80th percentile increased from $50,992 to $62,991. Nonetheless, even for these high-income families growth was much slower in these years than during the two decades after World War II.

The second summary measure of inequality is the share of income received by those in each of the five income quintiles. Families are ranked by income from poorest to richest and divided into five groups, each with the same number of families. Then the total income received by all families in each of these quintiles is expressed as a percentage of aggregate family income. For example, in 1991 the poorest fifth of families received 4.5 percent of total family income, while the richest fifth received 44.2 percent. According to this measure, the mean income of families in the richest quintile was almost ten times that of families in the poorest quintile.[8]

Table 3.1 shows the income shares of the five quintiles for selected years between 1947 and 1991, and Figure 3.4 charts the sum of the shares of the poorest two quintiles over the entire forty-year

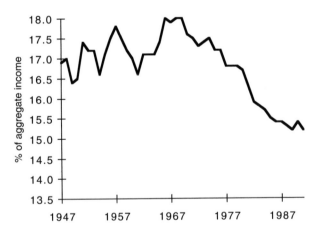

Figure 3.4   Share of aggregate income received by bottom 40 percent of families, 1947–1991. (Source: U.S. Bureau of the Census, Current Population Reports, ser. P-60.)

period. The pattern here is similar to that shown in Figure 3.2. Between 1947 and 1969 the income shares of each of the four bottom quintiles increased, and that of the top quintile declined. After 1969, however, the shares of the bottom three quintiles dropped, while that of the richest quintile reached a post–World War II high. For example, between 1969 and 1989 the income share of the poorest quintiles fell from 18.0 to 15.2 percent, a decline of 18 percent.

In 1991 the average income of the poorest fifth of families was $9,734. If inequality had not increased after 1969 and they had received the same income share in 1991 as in that year (5.6 percent), their average income would have been $12,106, or 24 percent higher. Likewise, in 1991 the richest fifth of families received 44.2 percent of total income and averaged $95,530. If their share in 1991 had been at 40.6 percent, as in 1969, their average income would have been $87,771, or 8 percent lower. This has been a period of both slow average growth and rising inequality.

Note also that all of the increased inequality between 1982 and 1989 was accounted for by the income gains of the richest 5 percent of families (see the last column of Table 3.1). Their share of total family income increased from 16.0 to 17.9 percent. Thus the richest 5 percent of families receives more total income than the bottom 40 percent.

The middle class has also fared relatively badly over the past two decades. The income shares of the second and third quintiles were lower in the late 1980s and early 1990s than in any other period after World War II. The income share of the middle quintile fell from 17.7 percent of total family income in 1969 to 16.5 percent in 1989.

That the middle class has fared badly over the recent past is central to our argument that the problems of poverty and inequality are primarily due to economic forces rather than to social policies or personal behavior. For example, consider middle-class married-couple families with children. These families are not welfare recipients and represent mainstream family structure. In 1989 the second quintile of married-couple families had an average income of $28,660, only 5 percent above the 1973 mean for this quintile. And, as we will discuss later, much of the growth in the incomes of married-couple families was accounted for by the increased wage rates and work effort of wives, not the rising wages of husbands.

Most of the increase in the share of the richest quintile occurred after 1981. Their gains were even larger than those indicated in Table 3.1, because the CPS data do not subtract taxes from income. Gramlich, Kasten, and Sammartino (1993) have constructed a post-tax distribution of income for the 1980s. In any year, federal income and payroll taxes paid are slightly progressive—that is, they raise the income shares of those at the bottom of the income distribution and lower the shares of those at the top. However, the tax cuts of 1981 particularly benefited the highest-income families. As a result, in the 1980s inequality in the post-tax distribution of income increased even more than inequality in pre-tax income.[9]

For more than twenty years, income inequality has increased during recoveries as well as during recessions. By the early 1980s inequality had increased to a level greater than that in any year back to 1947. Inequality continued to increase, reaching its highest level of the forty years in 1989. Thus almost all of the rise in inequality since World War II occurred during the 1980s. This explains the shift in conventional wisdom that we discussed in Chapter 1.

In the entire period since World War II, the 1980s stand out as a historical anomaly, a period of both rising family incomes and rising inequality. Part of these increases can be attributed to two recessions—January–July 1980 and July 1981–November 1982. Inequality typically increases during recessions, as employers retain the most-experienced workers when demand declines. The newly trained and the least-skilled, who have below-average earnings, are laid off and suffer the largest percentage losses of earnings as unemployment rises. During recoveries, in contrast, inequality usually declines as employers rehire laid-off workers and hire new ones. It was the continued sharp increase in inequality during the recovery of the 1980s that challenged the conventional wisdom. As we will show, this pattern of rising inequality plays a central role in explaining the continuing high poverty rates of the 1980s.

Our adjusted measure of family income—mean adjusted family income divided by the poverty line—yields a similar pattern of changes in the level and distribution of income, as shown in Table 3.3. According to this measure, a rising tide of rapidly growing incomes lifted individuals in all deciles, or tenths, of the income distribution between 1949 and 1969; then slower growth and an uneven tide, in which the poorest families lost and the richest ones gained, characterized the years between 1973 and 1991. Thus the rising inequality of the past two decades remains after we modify the census data to incorporate unrelated individuals and adjust for changes in family size.

For example, between 1949 and 1969 the mean income of persons in the fifth decile roughly doubled from 1.12 times to 2.31 times the poverty line, and growth was even more dramatic in the lowest four deciles. This pattern was reversed, however, between 1973 and 1991, when incomes grew more slowly in every decile

Table 3.3   Mean adjusted income divided by the poverty line, by decile of persons, selected years, 1949–1991

Decile	1949[a]	1969[a]	% change	1973[b]	1991[b]	% change
Lowest	0.07	0.39	+457.1	0.58	0.47	−19.0
2	0.38	1.02	+168.4	1.24	1.14	−8.1
3	0.65	1.50	+130.8	1.74	1.72	−1.1
4	0.89	1.91	+114.6	2.19	2.28	+4.1
5	1.12	2.31	+106.3	2.61	2.86	+9.6
6	1.35	2.73	+102.2	3.07	3.46	+12.7
7	1.62	3.22	+99.8	3.60	4.16	+15.6
8	1.97	3.84	+94.9	4.27	5.03	+17.8
9	2.50	4.82	+92.8	5.29	6.39	+20.8
Highest	4.15	8.39	+102.2	8.62	10.47	+21.5
Mean	1.47	3.01	+104.8	3.32	3.80	+14.5
Median	1.24	2.51	+102.4	2.84	3.14	+10.6

Source: See Table 3.2.

Note: Our measure of mean adjusted income divided by the poverty line is adjusted for inflation. In 1991 the poorest 10 percent of individuals lived in families where the ratio of family income to the poverty line was only 47 percent of the poverty line; the richest 10 percent, where it was more than 10 times the poverty line.

a. Computed from Census data.

b. Computed from Current Population Survey data.

than in the two decades after World War II, and the fastest increases were in the top deciles. Those in the bottom three income deciles actually had lower incomes in 1991 than their counterparts had in 1973. And the income of the fifth decile grew by only 10 percent. Because the haves gained so much more than the have-nots, income inequality increased.

It should be clear by now why researchers have devoted so much attention in the past few years to inequality in incomes. It should be equally evident why the conventional wisdom circa 1980 about such inequality was incorrect. From the vantage point of the 1990s, inequality has been on an upward trend since the late 1960s, but from the perspective of the late 1970s and early 1980s, the overriding fact was that the level of inequality was virtually the same in 1979 as it had been in 1949. Henry Aaron used a colorful metaphor when he wrote that observing changes in income inequality "was like watching the grass grow" (1978, p. 17).

In later chapters we will focus on the following questions: Why has inequality been increasing since the late 1960s? In particular, why did it increase so much during the 1980s? To use Aaron's analogy, why did the grass grow on only one part of the lawn? Our emphasis will be on understanding the historical record. Given how often projections prove incorrect, we will not speculate about the future course of inequality except to ponder whether the economic recovery that began in the middle of 1991 will resemble that of the 1960s, in which inequality decreased, or that of the 1980s. Our conclusion will depend, to a great extent, on whether the changes in antipoverty policies that we propose in Chapter 8 are implemented.

The Poor and the Rich

The federal government adopted an official poverty line—that is, a level of income below which a family of a given size is considered to be poor—after the declaration of the War on Poverty. A number of scholarly studies have examined the suitability of the official concept of income and of the poverty line. Patricia Ruggles (1990), for example, concluded that the standard of living represented by the official poverty line is too low because the official line is based on pre-1960 consumption patterns, and that "poverty standards today, to be comparable in terms of their consumption implications to the original . . . thresholds, would have to be at least 50 percent higher than the official thresholds" (1990, p. 167).

Nevertheless, we have chosen to be conservative in our measurement of poverty by using the official poverty line. For 1991 it ranged from $6,532 for a single person over the age of 65 to $27,942 for a family of nine or more; the average threshold for a family of four was $13,924. (For more on the poverty line and details about the calculation of the official thresholds, see "A Note on the Data," page 177.) As we will show, poverty rates based on the official line remain higher than most analysts expected. If we revised the poverty thresholds as proposed by Ruggles, the poverty rate would be even higher.

Despite the controversies, the official measure of poverty has become an important social indicator. As James Tobin correctly predicted twenty-five years ago: "Adoption of a specific quantitative measure, however arbitrary and debatable, will have durable and far-reaching political consequences. Administrations will be judged by their success or failure in reducing the officially measured prevalence of poverty. So long as any family is found below the official poverty line, no politician will be able to claim victory in the War on Poverty or ignore the repeated solemn acknowledgements of society's obligation to its poorest members" (1970, p. 83).

The United States has no official definition of "the rich." Published data are available on the mean incomes or income shares of those in the top quintile of families and of the top 5 percent of families. These data, however, cannot be used to analyze the effects of changes in economic growth on the absolute well-being of the rich. By definition, 20 percent of the population will be in the top quintile no matter what happens to the aggregate level or the distribution of income. For example, if the richest one-fifth of families are counted as "rich," and if their incomes are fixed but the incomes of the other four-fifths fall, the *share* of income going to the richest fifth will rise. This will result in an increase in inequality but not in the proportion of families who are rich.

We define the rich, not as some fixed percentage of the population, but as those whose incomes exceed a given threshold. That is, we count as rich all persons living in families with income exceeding seven times their poverty line. (For a family of four in 1991, seven times the poverty line, as defined by the CPI-U-X1, was about $90,000.) This is analogous to the official definition of poverty, which counts as poor all persons below a certain threshold (by definition, one times the poverty line). Any such threshold for defining the rich is arbitrary. We experimented with other definitions, but setting the threshold at seven or eight or nine times the poverty line did not change the pattern of our results.[10]

The proportion of the population that is rich is affected by both the level and the distribution of income, but it will not increase unless the absolute real incomes of the rich increase. For example, if every family's income doubled, there would be no change in income inequality, but poverty would decline and the percentage who were rich would increase. If, in contrast, the incomes of most families stayed constant but the incomes of those near the top of the distribution increased, there would be no change in poverty, but inequality and the percentage rich would increase.

Table 3.4 presents the percentage of persons who were poor and the percentage who were rich, according to our measures, for selected years from 1949 through 1991.[11] During the rapid growth of the postwar period, the poverty rate fell dramatically: from about 40 percent of all persons in 1949, to 22 percent in 1959, to 14 percent in 1969. In the same period, the rich increased from less than 1 percent of the population to more than 5 percent. Because the proportion who were poor fell so much more than the proportion who were rich grew, the middle class, according to this measure, also grew rapidly, from 60 percent in 1949 to 80 percent in 1969. (There is no agreed-upon definition of the middle class; we simply refer to anyone who is not rich or poor according to our measures— that is, those living in families with incomes between one and seven times the poverty line—as middle class.)

Figure 3.5 charts income divided by the poverty line for 1949 and 1969. Because real incomes in the late 1940s were on average less than half of those today, a large percentage of the population lived in families whose income divided by the poverty line was less than 2.0. Figure 3.5 categorizes all families in 1949 and 1969 into ten income groups, with each group representing one multiple of the

Table 3.4 The poor and the rich, selected years, 1949–1991

Year	Percentage of all persons	
	Poor[a]	Rich[b]
Census data		
1949	39.7	0.5
1959	22.3	2.4
1969	14.4	5.1
1979	13.1	7.4
Current Population Survey data		
1969 (P)	11.9	4.4
1971 (T)	12.1	5.0
1973 (P)	10.7	6.4
1975 (T)	11.2	5.1
1979 (P)	10.3	7.9
1982 (T)	12.9	8.0
1989 (P)	11.2	13.1
1991 (T)	12.5	11.7

Source: See Table 3.2.
Note: The Census data and the CPS data are not directly comparable, which is why poverty rates and the percentage rich differ for the two data sets in 1969 and 1979. The years of the business cycle peak and trough are indicated by (P) and (T).
a. Income is less than the CPI-U-X1 poverty line.
b. Income is more than seven times the CPI-U-X1 poverty line.

poverty line. In 1949 39.7 percent of the population lived in families with incomes below the poverty line; in 1969, 14.4 percent of the population was poor.

The shaded bars in Figure 3.5 show the difference between 1969 and 1949 for each category. Thus the first bar is at −25.3 and the second is at −13.9, indicating a large drop in the percentage of persons below the poverty line and with incomes between the poverty line and twice the poverty line. A larger portion of the population was in each of the eight higher ranges in 1969 than in 1949. In other words, as incomes grew rapidly throughout the income distribution (see Table 3.3), there were fewer poor and near-poor families, more in the middle-income ranges, and more among the rich.

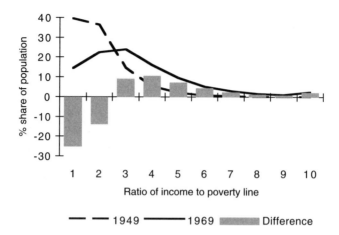

Figure 3.5 Distribution of income to needs, all persons, 1949 and 1969. The numbers below the line are the upper range of the income categories. Thus 3 represents persons living in families with incomes between two and three times the poverty line. (Source: Authors' calculations from 1950 and 1970 Decennial Censuses.)

For example, the three largest increases were in the middle-income categories between two and five times the poverty line. Figure 3.5 charts the essence of what it means to say that a rising tide lifts all boats: all income groups benefited from rapid economic growth.

Figure 3.6 and the bottom panel of Table 3.4 indicate that progress against poverty ended in the early 1970s even while the ranks of the rich continued to grow. The poverty rate in 1991 was 12.5 percent, 1.8 percentage points above the 1973 rate of 10.7 percent. Meanwhile, the ranks of the rich increased from 6.4 to 11.7 percent.

While Figure 3.5 showed the entire distribution moving toward higher income levels between 1949 and 1969, Figure 3.6 shows a distribution that has pulled apart from the middle. Instead of moving toward higher incomes, the mode remains centered at about three times the poverty line, there are fewer families in the middle ranges, and the upper and lower tails have grown. For example, in 1991 17.5 percent of persons had incomes between two and three times the poverty line, 5.6 percentage points fewer than in 1973.

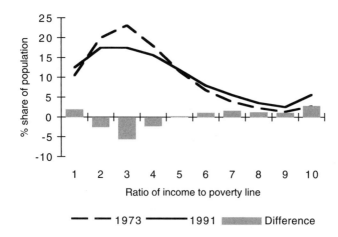

Figure 3.6 Distribution of income to needs, all persons, 1973 and 1991. (Source: Authors' calculations from March 1974 and March 1992 Current Population Surveys.)

The largest increases were for families in the four highest income categories.

The poverty rate tended to rise and fall with the strength of the business cycle until the recent period (see Table 3.4). It rose slightly during the 1969–1970 recession, then fell during the recovery. Despite the stagflation of the 1970s, the poverty rate fluctuated in a narrow range, and was as low at the 1979 peak of the business cycle as it had been at the 1973 peak. It increased from 10.3 to 12.9 percent in the recessions between 1979 and 1982, declined by only 1.7 percentage points during the seven-year recovery of the 1980s, and rose again to 12.5 percent by 1991. Poverty increased more during the recessions and declined less during the recovery than in earlier business cycles.

This simple relationship between the poverty rate and the state of the economy tells only part of the story. Economic growth does matter, but it matters less to the trend in poverty now than it did in the past (Gottschalk and Danziger, 1985; Blank, 1993), because the poverty rate reflects changes not only in average living standards but also in the shape of the income distribution. The trend in poverty mirrors the trend in median family income only when inequality is relatively constant.

It is not a question of whether poverty rates decline during a recovery, but of whether the declines are commensurate with the economy's growth. One way to evaluate the role of economic growth is to compare poverty rates with what they would have been if everyone had benefited roughly equally from the recovery. If the benefits of growth are no longer equally shared, then policymakers need to focus not only on growth but also on the distribution of the fruits of growth.

If inequality had remained constant, the incomes of all families would have grown at the same rate during each period. The poverty rate would have declined rapidly before 1973, stagnated during the 1970s, and risen during the 1982 recession. The trend in poverty did roughly follow this pattern, indicating that changes in inequality were less important than changes in the mean level of income. The poverty rate, however, should have declined significantly after 1982 and fallen to a new low by 1989, when median incomes reached a new peak (see Table 3.2). This did not happen because the relationship between economic growth and the poverty rate changed.

Figure 3.7 plots median family income (from Table 3.1) and the official poverty rate (from Table 3.5). The figure dramatically shows the erratic trend of poverty rates from 1965 to 1991. During the 1960s and 1970s median incomes tended to increase and poverty to decline: the poverty rate fell from 17.3 percent in 1965 to 11.4 percent in 1978 as median family income increased from $26,560 to $34,156.

The period 1979–1983, however, showed a very different pattern: median income fell and poverty rates rose along a new trajectory, reaching levels of poverty not seen since the mid-1960s. While the subsequent six-year expansion raised median incomes to unprecedented levels by 1989, poverty rates remained high. If poverty had fallen back along the path of the 1979–1983 data, it would have been about 10 percent in 1989 instead of almost 13 percent. The recession of the early 1980s seems to have altered the relationship between median family income and poverty.

Suppose the economy stays on the trajectory indicated in Figure 3.7. How much growth would it take to get poverty rates back

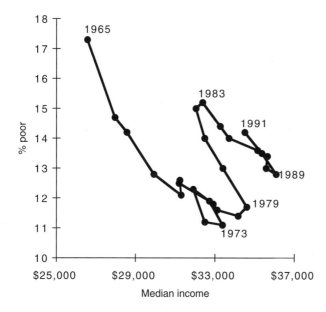

Figure 3.7 Poverty rate and median income, 1965–1991. Median income in 1990 dollars. (Source: U.S. Bureau of the Census, Current Population Reports, ser. P-60.)

to the 1973 level? Simply extrapolating along this trajectory indicates that median family income would have to grow to $39,000 (or over 13 percent). While this calculation is crude, it does indicate that, without dramatic changes in underlying demographic and economic factors, poverty will remain well above the level achieved in 1973. (See Chapter 5 for more on the role of economic and demographic changes in determining trends in poverty.)

A related point is worth noting. The U.S. poverty rate is particularly high relative to those of other industrialized countries with similar standards of living. Smeeding (1992) has gathered similar data sets from a number of countries and estimated poverty rates in a consistent manner. For the mid-1980s he finds poverty rates of around 13 percent in the United States, about 7 percent in Canada and Australia, 5 percent in France and the United Kingdom, and 4 percent or less in Sweden, Germany, and the Netherlands. Inequality in earnings and in family income are also higher in the

Table 3.5　Alternative measures of the trend in poverty, selected years, 1959–1991

Year	Percentage poor under official measure (1)	Adding noncash income and subtracting taxes (2)	Official measure using alternative adjustment for inflation (3)	Cumulative effect of columns 2 and 3 (4)
1959	22.4%	—	—	—
1964	19.0	—	—	—
1969	12.1	—	11.9%	—
1974	11.2	—	10.5	—
1979	11.7	8.9%	10.5	7.9%
1984	14.4	12.0	12.8	10.4
1989	12.8	10.4	11.4	8.9
1991	14.2	11.4	12.7	9.9

Source: U.S. Bureau of the Census, Current Population Reports, ser. P-60. This table contains information on selected years; data from every year in the Census Bureau publications are used in Figures 3.7 and 3.8.

Note: Column (2) counts government cash and noncash transfers, realized capital gains, and employer-provided health insurance as income and subtracts federal and state income taxes and payroll taxes from income; column (3) uses the experimental CPI to adjust the poverty thresholds; column (4) combines the effects of columns (2) and (3).

United States than in these other countries (see Chapter 6). These countries, like the United States, have experienced slower economic growth in the recent past than in the quarter-century following World War II; but they have avoided a rising rate of poverty and increased inequality by devoting more attention and more national resources to labor market and antipoverty policies than we have (see Hanratty and Blank, 1992; Blank and Hanratty, 1993; Jäntti and Danziger, 1994).

Adjustments to the Official Poverty Measure

Up to this point we have analyzed measures based on money income as defined by the Census Bureau. While there are problems with this concept of income, they do not affect our major conclusion—that the economic performance of the past two decades has been disappointing, especially for our poorest citizens. We now turn to several alternative Census Bureau measures of poverty to show that the finding that poverty has not declined over the past two decades is not an artifact of the particular income measures we use.

The official poverty rate, based on money income, does not reflect the value of in-kind benefits such as Food Stamps, Medicare, employer-provided health insurance, or public housing. Leaving these out of the calculation results in a higher poverty rate. When the official definition of poverty was developed, the poor received few such benefits, so comparing cash income to the poverty line provided a fairly accurate picture of a family's situation. However, in-kind transfers have grown rapidly in recent years, so omitting them from the calculation skews the poverty rate upward.

The official measure also does not take taxes into account. Taxes paid by the poor, especially payroll taxes, have increased in recent years (up to the late 1980s). Excluding them from the calculation lowers the measured poverty rate. Because the poor receive substantially more in in-kind benefits than they pay in taxes, however, the net effect of including both in-kind transfers and taxes is to lower the poverty rate in any year.

Table 3.5 and Figure 3.8 present the percentages of the population who were poor according to the official definition for the years 1959–1991 and according to several alternative definitions for shorter time spans. Column 2 of the table shows the poverty rate adjusted to reflect in-kind benefits and taxes. According to these adjusted data, 11.4 percent of the population, or 28.5 million persons, were poor in 1991. This is 2.8 percentage points, or about 7.2 million people, below the official rate for that year.

Nonetheless, while including in-kind transfers and taxes lowers the poverty rate, it does not affect the trend. The official poverty rates and the rates adjusted for in-kind transfers and taxes show very similar patterns over the period 1979–1991 (see Figure 3.8). In both series, poverty rose from 1979 to a post-recessionary high in 1983 and then fell gradually through the 1989 peak of the business cycle. In both series, the 1989 rate was higher than the rate during

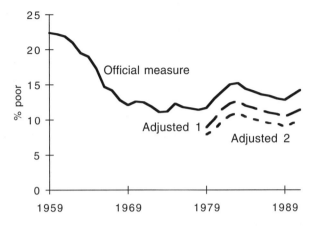

Figure 3.8 Poverty rates under alternative measures, 1959–1991. The top line shows the poverty rate under the official measure; the middle line, the rate as adjusted for noncash income and federal taxes; the bottom line, the rate as adjusted for noncash income, federal taxes, and an alternative inflation adjustment. (Source: U.S. Bureau of the Census, Current Population Reports, ser. P-60.)

the previous business cycle peak in 1979. Both rates rose after 1991 because of recession.[12]

Column 3 of Table 3.5 presents, for the period 1969–1991, a measure that indexes the poverty threshold by the CPI-U-X1, as does our adjusted measure. The official measure was not indexed by the CPI-U-X1 until 1983. By 1991 the CPI-U-X1 poverty rate, 12.7 percent, was 1.5 percentage points lower than the official rate. Combining the adjustments shown in columns 2 and 3—that is, using the CPI-U-X1 poverty line instead of the official line (for a family of four, for example, $12,667 instead of $13,924) and including the value of in-kind transfers—yields an even lower poverty rate, as shown in column 4 and in Figure 3.8. Calculating the poverty rate in this way yields a rate of 9.9 percent for 1991, higher than the 7.9 percent it yields for 1979.[13]

Several other types of adjustments would raise the poverty rate. The official poverty counts do not include homeless persons or those living in institutions, such as jails, prisons, and mental hospitals. Both these groups grew during the 1980s (U.S. Bureau of the Census, 1991b). While estimates of the number of homeless persons are imprecise, Burt (1992) suggests that there were roughly one-half million in the late 1980s. The number in jails and prisons increased by about one-half million during the 1980s. Including an additional million persons would raise the increase in poverty over the 1979–1989 period in any series shown in Table 3.5 by about 0.4 percentage points. Other changes that could increase the poverty rate include reestimating the poverty threshold and using different equivalence scales for the elderly (Ruggles, 1990).

Summary

Our review of more than four decades of data on average family income, income inequality, and poverty, using a variety of measures, shows that different forces were at work in different periods.[14] Before 1973, average family incomes grew rapidly, income inequality declined modestly, and the poverty rate dropped dramatically. The years between 1973 and 1979 were marked by stagnation in mean income and modest cyclical changes in inequality. The result was little improvement in living standards and only modest changes in the poverty rate. The rapid increase in poverty between 1979 and 1983 was due to back-to-back recessions, which produced falling average incomes and rising inequality.

It is the post-1983 period that is the anomaly. During this period mean income increased, but so did inequality. These two forces counteracted each other—by itself the rising mean should have led to an all-time low poverty rate. It was the rapid rise in inequality that not only prevented the poverty rate from reaching new lows but kept it above the 1973 level.

Macroeconomic conditions since the mid-1970s have refuted the two key assumptions that, for most of the past forty years, guided antipoverty policy and views about economic growth and inequality. The conventional wisdom at the beginning of the War on Poverty was that poverty could be alleviated by healthy economic growth, which could be achieved through macroeconomic control of the business cycle. This was a reasonable assumption in the mid-

1960s, as median family income had grown almost every year since the late 1940s. It was also believed that in an economy with low unemployment and with antidiscrimination policies and education and training programs in place, everyone—poor, middle class, and rich—would gain. At a minimum, it was expected that economic growth would be proportional and that all incomes would rise at about the same rate. At best, income growth for the poor would exceed the average rate, and poverty and inequality would continue to fall as they had in the preceding decades.

The first assumption proved wrong during the "quiet depression," which began in 1973 and lasted for a decade. When President Reagan took office he set out to get the economy moving again, just as President Kennedy had done after his election. The Reagan administration blamed the stagnation of the 1970s on the oil price shocks and President Carter's management of the economy. It assumed both that it could restore rapid economic growth and that a rising tide would still lift all boats.

In retrospect it is clear that both these assumptions were proved invalid in the 1980s. First, there was a long economic recovery, but total gains in income were modest and mostly resulted from increased work effort rather than rising real wage rates. Second, the economic growth had uneven distributional effects.

Where does this leave us in the mid-1990s? How can poverty and inequality be reduced in an environment of slow and unbalanced growth in family incomes? We address this issue in detail in Chapter 8. The experience of the past two decades suggests that economic growth alone will not be sufficient. If the original vision of the planners of the War on Poverty—an end to the American paradox of poverty amid plenty—is ever to be realized, a new set of antipoverty policies will be required.

Chapter 4

Demographic Groups with Persisting Disadvantages

Median incomes and poverty rates vary widely by race and ethnicity, by age, and by gender. During the 1950s and 1960s the economic circumstances of these groups converged somewhat; that is, income tended to grow and the rate of poverty tended to fall more rapidly for the poorest groups. The past twenty years, however, have been characterized by divergence among groups, with some of the lowest-income groups having the slowest growth in living standards and the largest increases in poverty.

Demographic Differences

The data for all persons, shown in Chapter 3, mask some dramatic differences. In any year, non-Hispanic whites are better off (that is, they have a higher median standard of living and a lower poverty rate) than blacks, Hispanics, and other minorities; nonelderly adults are better off than children and the elderly; married-couple families are better off than female-headed families; workers with more education are better off than those with less education. For example, current poverty rates for minorities and persons living in families headed by unmarried women are above 25 percent, higher than the 1959 poverty rate for all persons. And some groups—black children, Hispanic children, and white children living in mother-only families—have poverty rates as high as the 1949 rate for all persons, 40 percent.

With one major exception, these disparities among demographic groups have persisted over the past forty-five years. The exception is that until 1973 the poverty rate for the elderly was higher than that for children, whereas the poverty rate for children has been higher since 1973—and substantially higher in the 1990s (see Figure 4.1). Children's standards of living have been negatively affected by the uneven tides of the economy, by changes in public policies, and by demographic changes. That is, just when their fathers' real wages stopped increasing, policy changes also reduced their social safety net, and more and more of them lived in one-parent rather than two-parent families.

Over the past two decades only one demographic group has experienced rising incomes and substantial declines in poverty: the elderly. As we will show, however, the elderly have fared so well not primarily because of economic growth but rather because of rising government spending on their behalf. Their social safety net has been made increasingly secure so that the living standards of most of the elderly are no longer threatened by recessions or slow growth of the economy.

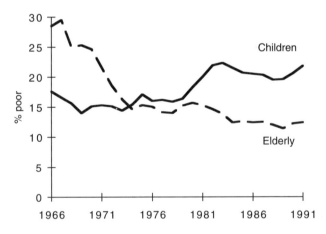

Figure 4.1   Poverty rates: children and the elderly, 1966–1991. "Children" refers to related children in families. "Elderly" refers to persons 65 and over. (Source: U.S. Bureau of the Census, Current Population Reports, ser. P-60.)

The recent period has also been characterized by a major economic shift within families. Because women's earnings have increased relative to those of men, and because more married women now work, the growth of family income depends less on higher wages for husbands and more on increased hours of work and higher wages for wives. During the post–World War II boom, a typical nonelderly family enjoyed a rising standard of living based on the rising earnings of a single breadwinner. While not all families in the 1950s and 1960s resembled television's Ozzie and Harriet family, the stereotype of a family achieving a middle-class lifestyle with a father working in the marketplace and a mother working at home was a much more accurate portrayal of the typical American family than it is in the 1990s.

The economic changes of the past two decades, however, have hit working men particularly hard. Their rising earnings are no longer the primary source of rising family living standards. Men's earnings, adjusted for inflation, increased dramatically between the late 1940s and the early 1970s, but then stopped growing. In fact, their real earnings were lower in 1991 than in 1973.[1] As a result, many families have relied on increased work effort to raise their standard of living. This most often means that the wife either enters the labor force or expands her hours of market work.

The economy has fluctuated in the years since World War II, but one major demographic change has been consistent: in each successive decade a smaller percentage of the population has lived in families headed by nonelderly, non-Hispanic white men. (In our empirical work we classify all persons into four racial/ethnic groups—white non-Hispanics, black non-Hispanics, Hispanics, and non-Hispanics of other races; in our tables we show detailed data for only the first three categories. For further discussion see "A Note on the Data," page 177. In the text we will refer to white non-Hispanics as "whites" and black non-Hispanics as "blacks.") Meanwhile, increasing proportions of the population belong to groups with lower-than-average living standards and higher-than-average poverty rates—female-headed families and minorities. If everything else remained constant, such a demographic shift would lower measures of economic progress for the population as a whole. But because families headed by nonelderly, non-Hispanic white men are still the largest group, the aggregate trends in living standards and poverty rates still primarily reflect their experience.

All groups, except the elderly, have experienced increased poverty and inequality in the past two decades. Because of demographic changes, the median income for all families has grown somewhat less than it would have otherwise, and the poverty rate is somewhat higher. The data we review in this chapter indicates, however, that the worsening economic hardship of the past two decades cannot be primarily attributed to the "decline of the American family" or to the relative increase in the size of the minority population. Economic progress during the past two decades would have been disappointing relative to that of the two decades after World War II even if there had been no demographic change. And even less progress would have occurred if women had not so rapidly increased their contributions to family income.[2] The role of government has also changed in the recent past: government programs have provided less cash assistance to many low-income families— except for the elderly—at a time when market forces have increased their need for such help.

Median Standards of Living

Table 4.1 shows median adjusted income divided by the poverty line for all persons and for various demographic groups.[3] In the top panel of the table, all persons are classified as living in families where the head is a nonelderly man, a nonelderly woman, or an elderly person;[4] in the bottom panel, as living in a family headed by a white non-Hispanic, a black non-Hispanic, or a Hispanic person. (In the rest of this discussion we will abbreviate certain cumbersome phrases: for example, we will use "families headed by women" or "female-headed families" as shorthand for "persons living in families headed by nonelderly women," and "elderly" for "persons living in families with elderly heads.")

Economic progress was very rapid for all demographic groups in the two decades after World War II, but quite modest in the 1970s and 1980s. Between 1949 and 1969 the median adjusted income of all of the six groups shown just about doubled. Income grew

Table 4.1 Median adjusted family income divided by the poverty line, for selected demographic groups[a]

Year	All persons	Persons living in families headed by			Ratio of medians	
		Nonelderly men	Nonelderly women	Elderly persons	Nonelderly women to nonelderly men	Elderly to all persons
1949	1.24	1.31	0.69	0.75	0.53	0.60
1969	2.51	2.76	1.36	1.78	0.49	0.70
% change	102.4%	110.7%	97.1%	137.3%		
1973	2.84	3.13	1.45	2.00	0.46	0.70
1991	3.14	3.63	1.64	2.68	0.45	0.85
% change	10.6%	16.0%	13.1%	34.0%		

Year	All persons	Persons living in families headed by a person who is[b]			Ratio of medians	
		White	Black	Hispanic	Black to white	Hispanic to white
1949	1.24	1.33	0.54	0.71	0.41	0.53
1969	2.51	2.74	1.44	1.62	0.53	0.59
% change	102.4%	106.2%	166.7%	128.2%		
1973	2.84	3.07	1.59	1.84	0.52	0.60
1991	3.14	3.54	1.85	1.83	0.52	0.52
% change	10.6%	15.3%	16.4%	-0.5%		

Source: See Table 3.2.

a. The median, computed separately for each group, is defined as family income/poverty line and weighted by the number of persons in the family. An unrelated individual is treated as a family of one person.

b. Persons who are not in a family headed by a member of one of these three groups are included in the totals for all persons. This group includes Asian-Americans, Native Americans, and other groups. The "other" category increased from 0.3 to 3.5 percent of all persons from 1949 to 1991.

least for female-headed families—about 97 percent, as the median increased from 69 percent of the poverty line to 1.36 times the poverty line. Even so, the income of female-headed families grew much more between 1949 and 1969 than did that of *any* demographic group between 1973 and 1991. The total growth of median adjusted income over the latter period was only about 15 percent for most groups and only about 34 percent for the elderly, a sharp reduction relative to the earlier decades.

During both of these twenty-year periods families headed by elderly persons fared better than the population as a whole. In 1949, for example, the median income of those in this group was about three-quarters of the poverty line, or about 60 percent of that of the average American. By 1969, however, it had increased to 1.78 times the poverty line, or 70 percent of that of the average American. Between 1973 and 1991 the median adjusted income of such families increased by 34.0 percent, much more than did the median for all persons (10.6 percent), and by 1991 the median adjusted income for this group was 2.68 times the poverty line, or 85 percent of the median for the population as a whole.

Changes in the labor market made the long-term improvement in the economic position of the elderly relative to the rest of the population even more remarkable. Since World War II the nonelderly, particularly women, have worked more, while the elderly have worked substantially less because of more frequent and earlier retirement. For example, 46 percent of elderly family heads in 1949, 32 percent in 1969, and only 19 percent in 1991 reported any labor-market income. The standard of living of the elderly rose even as they worked less, primarily because of rising Social Security benefits but also because of rising incomes from property and private pensions.

During both twenty-year periods, families headed by women fared worse than those headed by men: the median adjusted income of female-headed families was 53 percent of that of male-headed families in 1949, 49 percent in 1969, and 45 percent in 1991. In 1991 the median income of those in female-headed families was 1.64 times the poverty line. Even thirty years earlier the typical American had been slightly better off than this: in 1959 the median for all persons was 1.86 times the poverty line (see Table 3.2). The relative economic well-being of families headed by women declined even as their work effort increased: 60 percent of female family heads reported labor-market earnings in 1949, 70 percent in 1969, and 72 percent in 1991.

Although blacks started from a much lower base, they fared better than whites in the boom years after World War II, as black family income grew faster than that of whites. Median adjusted income for black families was only about one-half of the poverty line in 1949, or 41 percent of that of white families. By 1969 it had risen to 1.44 times the poverty line, or about 53 percent of that of whites. This gap has not narrowed over the past twenty-five years (see Jaynes and Williams, 1989). In 1991, the median income divided by the poverty line for blacks, 1.85, was only 52 percent of that for whites, and was at the same level as that for the overall population in 1959.

One bright spot, not shown in Table 4.1, is that the economic well-being of black, nonelderly, two-parent families has continued to improve relative to that of similar white families. Median adjusted income for these black families was 44 percent of that of their white counterparts in 1949, 61 percent in 1969, and 71 percent in 1991. The ratio of black to white incomes for the population as a whole has lagged because the trend toward female-headed families has been more marked among blacks than among whites.

Hispanics have made no economic progress in the last two decades: their median adjusted family income was virtually the same in 1991 as in 1973—1.83 times the poverty line, or about the 1959 level for all Americans. Between 1949 and 1969, in contrast, median adjusted income grew somewhat faster for Hispanics than for whites. In that period the Hispanic median rose from 53 to 59 percent of that of whites; by 1991, however, it had fallen to 52 percent. In 1991 the median adjusted income was virtually identical for blacks and Hispanics.

There are at least two possible explanations for the declining relative economic position of Hispanics. One explanation attributes it to the recent influx of Hispanic immigrants. Immigrants tend to earn lower wages when they first enter the U.S. labor market; as they gain experience their wages tend to rise. If this explanation is correct, the recent immigration will *temporarily* lower the ratio of Hispanic to white median income. Another possibility is that rising Hispanic immigration and other changes have led to more labor-market discrimination against Hispanics or to less demand by employers for jobs traditionally held by Hispanics. To date, few researchers have attempted to sort out the importance of these and other possible explanations (see Melendez, 1992).

Even though median living standards have grown only modestly over the past two decades, the income of the median American is close to an all-time high: in 1991 it was 3.14 times the poverty line, well above the levels of 1949 and 1959. Many Americans, however, have living standards much closer to those of earlier generations. The median adjusted income of families headed by women, blacks, and Hispanics in 1991 was close to that achieved by the median American in 1959. Median adjusted income for all persons in 1959 was 1.86 times the poverty line; in 1991, as shown in Table 4.1, the medians for persons living in families headed by nonelderly women, blacks, and Hispanics were 1.64, 1.85, and 1.83 times the poverty line, respectively. The 1991 median adjusted income for these groups would have had to grow by about 40 percent just to achieve the 1969 median for all persons, 2.51 times the poverty line. This is twice as much income growth as these groups actually experienced over the past two decades.

Children fared as well as the typical American during the postwar era, but less well in the 1970s and 1980s. The trends for children differ from those for the population as a whole, because children tend to live in families headed by relatively young adults and, in recent years, have been more likely to live with one parent than with two. These trends are particularly significant for minority children.

Trends in the median standards of living for children in the three largest racial/ethnic groups are shown in Table 4.2.[5] Between 1949 and 1969 the median living standard of children in each racial/ethnic group doubled, keeping pace with that of their group as a whole. After 1973, however, children fared somewhat worse than others in their demographic groups (compare Tables 4.1 and 4.2):[6] while the median adjusted income for all whites increased

Table 4.2 Median adjusted family income divided by the poverty line, for children, classified by race and ethnicity[a]

Year	All persons	Children living in families headed by a person who is[b]			Ratio of medians: Children to all persons		
		White	Black	Hispanic	White	Black	Hispanic
1949	1.24	1.16	0.44	0.63	0.93	0.35	0.51
1969	2.51	2.44	1.20	1.41	0.97	0.48	0.56
% change	102.4%	110.3%	172.7%	123.8%			
1973	2.84	2.73	1.25	1.54	0.96	0.44	0.54
1991	3.14	3.01	1.25	1.37	0.96	0.40	0.44
% change	10.6%	10.3%	0.0%	−11.0%			

Source: See Table 3.2.

a. The median, computed separately for each group, is defined as family income/poverty line and weighted by the number of persons in the family.

b. Persons who are not in a family headed by a member of one of these three groups are included in the totals for all persons. This group includes Asian-Americans, Native Americans, and other groups.

by 15.3 percent, that for white children grew by only 10.3 percent; while the median for all blacks went up by 16.4 percent, that for black children did not increase at all; and while the median for all Hispanics fell by 0.5 percent, that for Hispanic children fell by 11 percent.

The divergence in economic well-being by race and ethnicity is even wider for children than it is for all persons. In 1991 the median standard of living of white children was 96 percent of that of all persons, while the corresponding figures for black and Hispanic children were only 40 and 44 percent, respectively. In 1991 the median black or Hispanic child lived in a family whose standard of living was about the same as that of all Americans in 1949—only 1.24 times the poverty line.

Changing Sources of Income

Not only the rate of economic growth but also the sources of family income in the 1970s and 1980s differed from those in the two decades after World War II. Table 4.3 presents information on sources of income for persons living in families headed by nonelderly men, nonelderly women, and the elderly. Panel A for each group decomposes total adjusted mean family income divided by the poverty line into its various sources. Three sources are available in the Census data for 1949, four for 1969, and six in the Current Population Survey data for the most recent years. Panel B shows how each income source contributed to changes in the mean family income over the periods 1949–1969 and 1973–1991.

Families Headed by Nonelderly Men

These families have above-average levels of income and are the group most affected by the business cycle and by structural changes in the economy (as opposed to changes in government income-transfer programs). In 1991 the earnings of the heads of these families accounted for 63.4 percent of total adjusted family income and the earnings of their wives for 21.5 percent.[7] The remaining 15 percent came from a variety of sources: earnings of other family members, 5.5 percent; property income (dividends, interest and rent),

3.5 percent; cash government transfers (Social Security, unemployment insurance, welfare, and so on), 4.1 percent; and all other income sources (private pensions, alimony, child support, and so on), 1.9 percent.

Such an examination of the sources of income reveals enduring facts as well as changes. For families headed by nonelderly men, the largest single source of income in every year is the earnings of the family head. Yet men's earnings declined in importance over these four decades, accounting for 82.7 percent of family income in 1949, about 75 percent in 1969 and 1973, and 63.4 percent in 1991. This decline reflects two trends: first, after the early 1970s the growth rate of men's earnings slowed; and second, over the entire period more wives have entered and remained in the labor force, and their wage rates and annual hours of work increased. The share of family income contributed by wives' earnings increased dramatically, from 8.5 percent in 1959 to 13.1 percent in 1969, and to 21.5 percent in 1991.

During the post–World War II boom, mean adjusted income divided by the poverty line for families headed by nonelderly men more than doubled, from 1.31 to 2.76 times the poverty line (see Table 4.1). As shown in panel B of Table 4.3, men's earnings were the primary engine of growth in family income, accounting for 67 percent of the increase. After 1973, however, the *absolute* level of earnings of nonelderly male heads stagnated. Men's earnings remained the largest source of family income, but accounted for only 2.5 percent of the growth in family income between 1973 and 1991. Wives' earnings grew so much faster than those of their husbands during this period that their earnings replaced those of men as the primary engine of growth in family income.

There is little evidence that the increased work effort of women was caused by the stagnation of men's earnings, or that it substantially affected the rate of growth of men's earnings. Married women's participation in the labor force began to increase in the 1950s, well before the growth in men's earnings tapered off. Moreover, the labor force participation of women married to men with above-average earnings grew faster than that of all married women. Working wives were the most important source of income growth

Table 4.3 Sources of change in mean adjusted family income divided by the poverty line

Persons living in families headed by	Head's earnings	Spouse's earnings	Earnings of others	Property income	Government transfers	All other sources
			Sources of income			
Nonelderly males						
A. Percentage of mean from each source						
1949	82.7	12.3			5.0	
1969	74.6	13.1	6.0		6.3	
1973	74.1	13.6	6.1	2.0	3.3	0.8
1991	63.4	21.5	5.5	3.5	4.1	1.9
B. Sources of change in mean						
1949–1969	67.3	25.3			7.4	
1973–1991	2.5	66.7	2.2	12.1	8.4	8.2
Nonelderly females						
A. Percentage of mean from each source						
1949	59.2		25.3		15.5	
1969	61.5		18.6		20.0	
1973	56.5		16.4	3.5	18.1	5.5
1991	66.9		13.0	3.3	10.3	6.5
B. Sources of change in mean						
1949–1969	64.1		10.6		25.3	
1973–1991	143.7		−12.1	1.5	−47.4	14.3

Elderly persons

A. Percentage of mean from each source

Year	Earnings	Wives'/others' earnings		Property income	Govt. transfers	Other	
1949	46.2	{ 26.9	}	{ 27.0			}
1969	23.5	6.1	16.1		52.6		
1973	16.0	5.7	15.0	13.2	43.1		
1991	9.9	4.4	10.9	17.2	47.5	7.2	10.1

B. Sources of change in mean

Period	Earnings	Wives'/others' earnings		Property income	Govt. transfers	Other
1949–1969	5.6	{ 18.4	}	{ 76.0		}
1973–1991	−12.2	−0.1	−4.1	32.0	63.7	20.8

Source: Authors' calculations based on data from Census Bureau computer tapes.

Note: Sources may not add across rows to 100.0 because of rounding. A negative sign in Panel B means that the absolute level of a given source declined over the period. The Census data do not allow us to distinguish between the earnings of wives and the earnings of others for 1949, or to separate property income, government transfers, and other sources for 1949. In such cases the table shows a bracketed figure that is the sum of the bracketed categories.

not just for the mean family shown in Table 4.3 but for families at all levels of income (see Cancian, Danziger, and Gottschalk, 1993a).

Over this period of slow growth in living standards, mean family income grew modestly (by about 17 percent), and 66.7 percent of the increase was due to the rising earnings of wives.[8] Wives' earnings averaged 0.47 times the poverty line in 1973 and 0.87 times by 1991. The remaining contributions to the rising mean in families headed by nonelderly men were rising property incomes (12.1 percent), rising government income transfers (8.4 percent), earnings of other family members (2.2 percent), and other sources (8.2 percent).

These results for families headed by nonelderly men are consistent with our view that adverse economic changes—in this case, the stagnation of men's earnings—rather than demographic changes are primarily responsible for the economic hardship now faced by many Americans. In the postwar era steady growth in men's earnings was the primary source of the increased standard of living, but over the past two decades their earnings, on average, have not contributed much to the small increase in their families' standards of living.

This shift from husbands' earnings to wives' earnings as the primary engine of improvement in family living standards is even more dramatic when we consider only families with children (the data in Table 4.3 include families with and without children). For families headed by nonelderly men and including children, growth in husbands' earnings accounted for 73 percent of the rapid growth in family income between 1949 and 1969, even though the proportion of married mothers with earnings doubled (from about one-fifth to two-fifths) during that period.

Between 1973 and 1991, however, the mean adjusted earnings of fathers in families with children actually declined slightly. Wives, meanwhile, continued to enter the labor force and to work longer hours: by 1991 two-thirds of all mothers in two-parent families had earnings. Mothers' earnings increased rapidly, both because more of them worked and because real earnings, on average, increased for working women. During this period, mothers' earnings accounted for 95 percent of the increase in their children's standard of living! In other words, children in male-headed families would have had a *lower* standard of living in 1991 than in 1973 if their mothers had not worked more and earned more over these two decades.

The two decades after 1973 were remarkable. On average, non-elderly men, and fathers in particular, were unable to improve their families' standards of living significantly. If any single factor exemplifies the shift from an era of rising tides to one of uneven tides, it is the stagnation in the earnings of men. Because this change is so important, we will devote Chapters 6 and 7 to an analysis of its causes and implications. We will demonstrate not only that mean male earnings have hardly grown over the past two decades but also that inequality in men's earnings has increased.

Families Headed by Nonelderly Women

The data on sources of income for nonelderly female household heads reveal some surprises. The conventional wisdom today is that many female household heads depend on welfare instead of working.[9] Contrary to this popular stereotype, however, our data show that the women's earnings are by far the most important source of income for these families. Female-headed families have low average incomes in spite of the significant work effort of women for several reasons: because they have fewer adults; because women's wage rates are lower than men's; and because these families receive relatively little cash assistance from government programs. The earnings of the female head made up about 60 percent of total family income divided by the poverty line in both 1949 and 1969. Over these two decades increases in their earnings accounted for 64 percent of the total growth in their families' income.

Government cash transfers have done relatively little to raise the living standards of female-headed families. Such transfers rose in the two decades after World War II, but accounted for at most 20 percent of these families' income in 1969. As the economy soured and wages grew more slowly after 1973, government benefits for female-headed families also lagged. Inflation eroded the real value of benefits and program changes made it harder to qualify for some benefits. Thus by 1991 government cash transfers amounted to only 10.3 percent of the mean adjusted income of families headed by women.

In the two decades after 1973, female family heads, like wives in two-parent families, were the primary source of income growth for their families. Between 1973 and 1991 the earnings of female family heads increased from 56.5 to 66.9 percent of family income, and accounted for 143.7 percent of the total growth in their families' income. Because of the falling absolute level of government transfers, the living standards of these families would have declined substantially had their heads not earned more.

These trends were similar for *children* living in female-headed families (detailed data not shown in the table). Between 1949 and 1969 the mean living standard of these children grew rapidly because both their mothers' earnings and government transfers were increasing. The proportion of mothers with earnings increased from 54 to 63 percent over this period, and their real earnings doubled. The rising earnings of mothers accounted for about two-thirds of the total growth in income; rising transfers and other income sources made up the remaining third.

Since the late 1960s, however, the work effort of female family heads with children has remained roughly constant. Although the growth of single mothers' earnings slowed down in this period, their mean earnings nevertheless increased by about one-half. In 1991, 63 percent of female heads with children had earnings, and their earnings accounted for 61.5 percent of their childrens' mean family income—a percentage quite similar to that provided by fathers' earnings in married-couple families.

Nevertheless, the total family income of these children is much lower than that of children in married-couple families. In single-parent families, there is rarely a second adult who helps support the family. Contributions from absent fathers to their children (in the form of child support and alimony) account for less than 10 percent of total family income. In two-parent families the earnings of wives have grown faster than those of husbands, and in mother-only families the mothers' earnings have grown faster than contributions from absent fathers in support of their children.[10]

The earnings of single mothers averaged 0.58 times the poverty line in 1973 and 0.86 times in 1991. If income from all other sources had remained at 1973 levels, this growth in earnings would have increased mean income for children in these families by 21 percent. However, children's incomes in mother-only families actually rose by only 7.5 percent in this period, primarily because the real value of government transfers declined. In 1973 cash transfers averaged 0.42 times the poverty line and accounted for 32 percent of income for mother-only families; by 1991 they averaged only 0.24 times the poverty line, or 17 percent of total adjusted family income.

Families Headed by Elderly Persons

The elderly have gained in income relative to other age groups over the past forty-five years despite a trend toward earlier retirement. In 1949, when Social Security benefits were much lower than they are now and far fewer elderly persons received benefits, the earnings of elderly family heads accounted for 46 percent of their families' income. Over the next twenty-five years the Social Security system matured and real benefits were increased, while the labor force participation of the elderly declined dramatically. By 1973 the earnings of elderly family heads accounted for only 16 percent of total family income, and by 1991 for only 9.9 percent.

Since World War II, rising government benefits have been the primary engine of family income growth for the elderly; by 1991 government transfers accounted for 47.5 percent of their total family income—slightly more than the share accounted for by the elderly heads' earnings in 1949. The growth of government transfers accounted for three-quarters of the rise in these families' income between 1949 and 1969, and for two-thirds of the rise between 1973 and 1991.

Social Security benefits have risen dramatically in real terms since 1949. They have grown relative to the median earnings of all male workers, relative to the poverty line, and relative to mean welfare benefits available to single-mother families with children. In 1950 the mean annual Social Security benefit for a retired male worker and his wife (in 1990 dollars) was $2,593. This amounted to about one-fifth of the median earnings of all male workers and about one-third of the poverty line for an elderly couple. By 1989 the mean benefit for such a couple had increased to $12,200 (again, in 1990 dollars), about two-thirds of median earnings of male workers and one and one-half times the couple's poverty line. Social Security benefits have also grown relative to welfare spending on families with children.

We assume that the poverty line represents a minimum annual retirement income for the elderly. Under this scenario, the average Social Security benefit can be viewed as having been transformed from a retirement supplement in the 1940s and 1950s to a minimum guaranteed income by 1970 and to something well beyond a minimum income by 1980 (see Smolensky, Danziger, and Gottschalk, 1988).[11]

For elderly persons who are not eligible for Social Security, or whose past earnings qualify them for only minimal benefits, the Supplemental Security Income program (SSI) now provides a guaranteed annual income. The enactment of SSI in October 1972 resulted from the long and futile effort by the Nixon administration to pass the Family Assistance Plan (FAP). Introduced in Congress in 1969, FAP was initially a negative income tax with universal coverage of families with children. The legislation was later expanded to include elderly, blind, and disabled persons. Although FAP passed the House twice, it never succeeded in the Senate. Only the part of the legislation that aided elderly, blind, and disabled persons—SSI—was enacted. If FAP had passed, children would now have the same income floor as the elderly.

The property income of families headed by elderly persons has rapidly increased, both absolutely and as a share of their total income. Income from property made up only 7 percent of the family income of the typical elderly person in 1969, but its share rose quickly to 17.2 percent by 1991. Much of this growth was due to the high real interest rates of the 1980s and the increasing financial assets of the elderly. Over the 1973–1991 period, the growth in property income accounted for about one-third of the increased family income of the elderly, while the growth in government transfers accounted for about two-thirds and growth in income from other sources—primarily private pensions—accounted for about one-fifth. Taken together, growth in these three types of income more than offset the declining earnings of the elderly in these two decades: their adjusted mean income divided by the poverty line grew twice as fast as that of the nonelderly, primarily because of increasingly generous government transfers.

Sources of Income for Racial and Ethnic Groups

An examination of changes in the sources of income by race and ethnicity (data not shown) reveals similar patterns for whites, blacks, and Hispanics. For each group, growth in men's earnings was the most important source of growth in total family income between 1949 and 1969. Between 1973 and 1991 there were some modest differences among these groups: for white families, wives' earnings were the most important source of income growth; for black families, husbands' and wives' earnings were equally important; and for Hispanic families, husbands' earnings fell but the earnings of wives and other workers in the families rose.

The median standard of living of minorities is much lower than that of the white majority. Because the view that anyone who works hard can get ahead is so widely held, many people attribute this difference in living standards to race-specific behavior. Our analysis, however, demonstrates that the slow growth and increasing inequality of the past two decades have had very similar effects on the living standards of whites and minorities. Therefore, the differences in income trends do not primarily reflect behavioral differences among the races; they reflect changes in the economy. Large gaps between the living standards of whites and those of other groups have persisted, but the *trends* over time have been quite similar for all racial/ethnic groups, as indicated in Figure 4.2.

Figure 4.2 plots the percentage of male high school graduates aged 25–34 whose annual earnings were less than the poverty line for a family of four.[12] In the economic boom that followed World War II, the percentage of high school graduates with low earnings dropped dramatically for whites, blacks, and Hispanics alike. Among whites, for example, in 1949, 33.9 percent of these young men earned less than the poverty line for a family of four. This is not surprising, since in 1949 the median white family's total income was only 1.33 times the poverty line (Table 4.1). As median family income rose to 2.74 times the poverty line in the next twenty years,

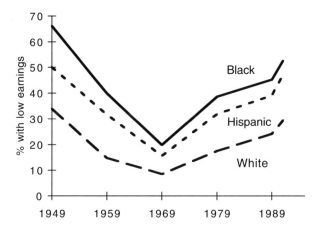

Figure 4.2   Percentage of male high school graduates aged 25–34 with earnings less than the poverty line for a family of four persons, 1949–1991. (Source: Authors' calculations from Census Bureau computer tapes.)

the earnings of white high school graduates also rose rapidly; by 1969 only 8.6 percent were low earners.

In the next two decades, as growth slowed and real earnings of high school graduates declined, the proportion of white high school graduates with low earnings rose sharply, and by 1991, 29.5 percent earned less than the poverty line for a family of four, a rate similar to that of the 1950s. Note that the young men facing this pattern of economic hardship are not from a stereotypical underclass of inner-city teenagers who have dropped out of high school. They have earned high school diplomas and are old enough to have more than a decade of potential labor force experience. Increasingly, over the past two decades, they have not been able to find "good jobs."

This pattern of rapidly falling and then rapidly rising rates of low earnings for male high school graduates is also evident for blacks and Hispanics. Figure 4.2 does show some narrowing in the gap between groups during the post–World War II boom, but the groups diverge again in the 1970s. The low earnings rate for Hispanic men was 16 percentage points higher than that for white men in 1949, fell to 7 points higher by 1969, and rose again to almost 18 points higher than the white rate by 1991. In a similar pattern, the rate for black men fell from 32.2 percentage points higher than that of white men in 1949 to 11.3 points higher in 1969, then rose to 23 points above the white rate by 1991.

Figure 4.2 focuses only on one group of high school graduates, controlling for age and education. Thus any remaining racial or ethnic difference in the low earnings rate is likely to be due to discrimination, differences in the ability to find jobs, or some unobserved personal characteristics such as ability or motivation (see Moss and Tilly, 1992, and Bound and Freeman, 1992, for a discussion of black/white earnings differences). The pattern shown in Figure 4.2, of falling rates of low earnings until the early 1970s and rising rates thereafter, also holds for men of other age and education cohorts and for women (see U.S. Bureau of the Census, 1992b).

In fact, rates of low earnings for young college graduates in 1991 were substantially above the 1969 rates for young high school graduates shown in Figure 4.2. The 1991 rates of low earnings for male college graduates aged 25–34 were 16.8 percent for whites, 24.7 percent for blacks, and 32.2 percent for Hispanics.

The similarities of the economic trends across racial and ethnic groups that we have documented in this chapter should not be underestimated. They clearly challenge the conventional wisdom that attributes the declining economic status of minorities primarily to their detachment from the labor force or their family structure. Such factors can explain a part of the gap in living standards between minorities and whites in any year, but they cannot account for much of the *increase* in economic hardship of the past two decades.[13] The increased rate of low earnings for white high school graduates between 1969 and 1991 has, by definition, nothing to do with the labor force behavior or family structure of minorities. We have also found that over the 1973–1991 period the mean earnings of black married-couple families rose from 65 to 71 percent of those of similar white families. Thus the primary cause of the diminished economic prospects over these two decades is to be found in economic changes that have buffeted all families, not in race-specific behavioral explanations.

Poverty

The demographic groups that have the highest median adjusted family incomes have the lowest poverty rates; groups with the fastest-growing family incomes have the fastest-falling poverty rates. Thus it should come as no surprise that poverty rates are lowest for persons living in families headed by nonelderly men and for whites, or that they have declined most rapidly for the elderly. Table 4.4 presents the poverty rates for the six demographic groups.

Between 1949 and 1969 the poverty rate declined dramatically for every group. It fell by about 26 percentage points for persons liv-

Table 4.4   Poverty rates, by age and gender and by race and ethnicity, selected years, 1949–1991

Year	All persons	Persons living in families headed by		
		Nonelderly men	Nonelderly women	Elderly
1949	39.65%	35.06%	60.01%	59.28%
1969	14.42	8.67	40.42	26.59
% change[a]	−25.23	−26.39	−19.59	−32.69
1973	10.65	5.78	36.12	15.91
1991	12.47	7.25	34.99	9.40
% change[a]	+1.82	+1.47	−1.13	−6.51

	All persons	Persons living in families headed by a person who is		
		White	Black	Hispanic
1949	39.65	35.26	75.41	65.26
1969	14.42	11.08	34.64	27.07
% change[a]	−25.23	−24.18	−40.77	−38.19
1973	10.65	7.19	30.52	20.40
1991	12.47	7.97	29.31	25.32
% change[a]	+1.82	+0.78	−1.21	+4.92

Source: See Table 3.2.

a. Percentage point difference between later year and earlier year poverty rates.

ing in families headed by nonelderly men, 20 points for those living with nonelderly women, 33 points for those living with the elderly, about 40 points for families headed by blacks and Hispanics, and about 24 points for those headed by whites. In 1949 persons living in families headed by blacks and Hispanics had the highest poverty rates, but by 1969 it was those in families headed by women: their poverty rate was 40 percent, compared with 35 percent for blacks and 27 percent for Hispanics.

Between 1973 and 1991, overall family income growth was slow and the poverty rate hardly changed at all for four of the demographic groups. It rose by about 5 percentage points for Hispanics and fell by about 7 points for the elderly. The 1991 poverty rates for those in families headed by blacks, Hispanics, and nonelderly women, at 29.3, 25.3, and 35.0 percent, respectively, were decades behind the rate for all persons: the rates for blacks and Hispanics were close to the overall rate for 1959 (22.3 percent), while that for female-headed families was close to the overall rate for 1949 (39.7 percent).

Children in Poverty

Table 4.5 presents poverty rates for all children and for children classified by the race and sex of the head of their family.[14] Poverty rates declined rapidly for all groups of children between 1949 and 1969. Between 1973 and 1991, however, poverty rates rose faster for children than for any other demographic group. One reason for this trend is that children's parents tend to be younger than other adults, and younger adults fared worse in the labor market than other adults after 1973. Another is that government benefits for families with children lagged behind those for other groups, especially the elderly.

Notice that the poverty rate for all children *rose* between 1973 and 1991. Classifying children by the racial/ethnic group and the sex of their family heads reveals different and somewhat offsetting trends in poverty. If male-headed and female-headed families are considered separately, poverty rates went down for black children in both groups and stayed level for Hispanic children in female-headed families. However, the increase in the proportion of children

Table 4.5   Child poverty rates, selected years, 1949–1991

	1949	1969	1973	1991
All children[a]	46.9%	14.9%	14.0%	19.7%
White	40.6	9.9	8.1	11.6
Black	86.7	41.2	39.4	42.4
Hispanic	72.9	31.2	26.5	35.5
White children living in families headed by				
Men	38.6	6.9	5.1	6.4
Women	72.1	42.2	36.5	39.3
Black children living in families headed by				
Men	85.0	29.9	20.8	15.3
Women	94.1	66.9	65.7	63.8
Hispanic children living in families headed by				
Men	71.2	27.2	16.0	24.6
Women	87.5	61.1	65.4	65.3

Source: See Table 3.2.

a. Children who are not in families headed by a member of one of these groups are included in the totals for all children. This group includes Asian-Americans, Native Americans, and other groups.

living in one-parent families (most of them in mother-only families) offset these within-gender declines, so that the overall poverty rate for children in each racial/ethnic group went up. The striking feature of Table 4.5, however, is how high poverty rates remained in 1991 for *all* groups of children except white children in male-headed families.

Because so much policy attention has been focused on the contrasting situations of children and the elderly, we should emphasize the implications of the divergent trends for these two groups. Many current policy discussions focus on the question of why the elderly have fared so much better than children. But we caution the reader not to conclude that most of the elderly are better off than most children.

In fact, the mean standards of living and the poverty rates of the elderly vary as widely by demographic group as do those of children. For example, the poverty rate for elderly persons living in families headed by white men was 4.5 percent in 1991, while that for children in families headed by white men was 6.4 percent. But the poverty rate for elderly blacks and Hispanics living in married-couple families was about twice that for these children, and the rates for persons in families headed by elderly women were 19.9 percent for whites, 44.9 percent for blacks, and 35.4 percent for Hispanics. At the same time, the poverty rate for white children living in mother-only families (39.3 percent) was much higher than the rate for black children living in families headed by men (15.3 percent).

The differences in economic well-being between children and the elderly can be traced to differences in sources of income. Most children live with nonelderly adults whose living standards are determined by real wage rates and unemployment rates. Most of the elderly are dependent on inflation-adjusted government benefits and are largely immune to the economy's business cycles. Minorities fare less well than whites because of their lower wages and higher unemployment. This lowers the economic well-being of minority children, but it also leads to lower Social Security benefits and private pensions for the minority elderly. Families headed by women fare less well than married-couple families because women earn less than men, because these families have fewer adult wage earners, and because their welfare benefits are low.

Consider the main government programs for poor children, Aid to Families with Dependent Children (AFDC) and Food Stamps.[15] Benefits from these programs vary by state; in the median state, the combined benefit from AFDC and Food Stamps in the early 1990s was only about 72 percent of the poverty line for a mother with two children. In addition, only about 60 percent of poor children now receive benefits.

In contrast, the elderly poor are eligible for the Supplemental Security Income (SSI) program, which is indexed for inflation and has a national minimum benefit level. In most states an elderly couple receive substantially more from SSI ($7,596 in 1991) than a mother and two children receive from AFDC (less than $5,000 in the median state).

In sum, child poverty would be much lower if children had access to the social safety net that serves the elderly. Nonetheless, to reduce poverty among those elderly subgroups with high poverty rates will require additional reforms in these programs.

As we have seen, demographic groups classified by age, sex, race, and ethnicity have diverse standards of living. Nonetheless, most have experienced similar economic fortunes over the past forty-five years. During the post–World War II boom years, family incomes rose and poverty and income inequality declined; after 1973, however, income growth slowed down, poverty rates stagnated, and inequality increased. White, black, and Hispanic men all found it harder to earn enough in the labor market to support their families.

Chapter 5

Why Poverty Remains High

There is a widespread tendency to blame demographic factors, such as increasing rates of divorce and out-of-wedlock childbearing, for the high poverty rates of recent years. Butler and Kondratas exemplify this position: "Poverty in the United States today is inextricably intertwined with family structure and the economic viability of families. Broken families lead to poverty . . . The connection between family and poverty—not racism—is the explanation for the high poverty rate of American blacks" (1987, pp. 139–140).

We do not agree that changes in family structure are the main reason poverty rates remain so high. While it is true that demographic shifts have contributed to the rise in the poverty rate, they have been less important than the economic changes that have accompanied them. As we will show in this chapter, income inequality increased within all demographic groups, and was at least as important as changes in the demographic composition of the population in accounting for the increased poverty. The major difference between the rapidly falling poverty rate of the post–World War II economic boom and the rising poverty rate of the past two decades is the latter period's much slower growth in living standards and its rising inequality of incomes.

Demographic Changes

The increase in the proportion of the U.S. population, and especially of the minority population, living in female-headed families has received substantial attention recently. This demographic change, however, actually began in the 1950s and accelerated in the 1970s.

Table 5.1 shows the composition of the population by age and gender (top panel) and by racial/ethnic group (bottom panel) of family heads. As in earlier chapters, we classify every family as headed by a nonelderly man, a nonelderly woman, or an elderly person; and we use three racial/ethnic classifications, white, black, and Hispanic. (For details of these classifications see "A Note on the Data," page 177.)

In 1949, as indicated in the top panel of the table, about four-fifths of all persons lived in families headed by nonelderly men, about 9 percent with nonelderly women, and another 11 percent with the elderly. Since that time the first group has declined in relative size as the other two have grown. The changes between 1949

Table 5.1   Changes in the demographic composition of the population, selected years, 1949–1991

| Year | Persons living in families headed by[a] | | |
	Nonelderly men	Nonelderly women	Elderly persons
1949	80.4	8.9	10.7
1969	77.7	10.9	11.4
1973	76.1	11.8	12.1
1991	68.1	17.3	14.6

| Year | Persons living in families headed by a person who is[b] | | |
	White	Black	Hispanic
1949	88.0	9.9	1.8
1969	85.5	11.1	2.3
1973	82.3	11.2	5.1
1991	75.4	12.2	8.9

Source: See Table 3.2.

a. An unrelated individual is counted as a one-person family.

b. Persons who are not a member of one of these three groups are included in the totals for all persons. This group includes Asian-Americans, Native Americans, and other groups. All persons within a family are classified according to the race/ethnicity of the head of the family.

and 1969 were rather modest: the portion of the population living in families headed by nonelderly women increased by 2 percentage points, and the portion living in families headed by elderly persons increased by less than 1 percentage point.

These trends accelerated in the 1970s: the share of the population living in families headed by nonelderly women increased by 5.5 percentage points between 1973 and 1991, to 17.3 percent. Over the same period, the share of the population living in families with elderly heads increased by 2.5 points, to 14.6 percent. Thus by 1991 only about two-thirds of the population lived in families headed by nonelderly men.

As indicated in the bottom panel of Table 5.1, the American population has become more racially and ethnically diverse since 1949. Between 1949 and 1991 the portion of the population living in families *not* headed by whites doubled, from 12 to 25 percent. The portion in families headed by blacks increased from 9.9 to 12.2 percent, while the portion in families headed by Hispanics increased fivefold, from 1.8 to 8.9 percent, with most of the increase occurring after 1969.[1] As a result, by 1991 one in four Americans lived in a family whose head was either black, Hispanic, or a member of another nonwhite group.

The living arrangements of children, as indicated in Table 5.2, changed even more than those of all persons. (For purposes of this discussion children are assumed to belong to the same racial/ethnic group as the head of their family.) In 1949, 5.9 percent of all white children lived in families headed by women. The proportion for Hispanic children was roughly twice as high (10.2 percent), and that for black children three times as high (18.9 percent). By 1991 these proportions had grown to 16 percent of white children, more than half of black children, and more than a quarter of Hispanic children. Furthermore, since these figures are based on cross-sectional data that measure living arrangements during a single year, the actual proportions of children who live in mother-only families at some time during their childhood are considerably higher (Bumpass and Sweet, 1989).

In 1949 most single-parent families were headed by women who had been married and were divorced, widowed, or separated. Few

Table 5.2 Changes in the living arrangements of children, selected years, 1949–1991

	1949	1969	1973	1991
All children[a]	100.0%	100.0%	100.0%	100.0%
White	85.5	82.1	77.5	68.8
Black	11.6	13.6	14.3	15.5
Hispanic	2.5	3.1	6.9	12.0
White children living in families headed by				
Males	94.1	91.5	90.5	84.0
Females	5.9	8.5	9.5	16.0
Never married	0.1	0.3	0.4	2.6
Divorced/separated/widowed	5.8	8.2	9.1	13.4
Black children living in families headed by				
Males	81.1	67.5	58.6	44.2
Females	18.9	32.5	41.4	55.8
Never married	1.0	5.3	8.0	27.2
Divorced/separated/widowed	17.9	27.2	33.4	28.6
Hispanic children living in families headed by				
Males	89.8	88.3	78.8	73.1
Females	10.2	11.7	21.2	26.9
Never married	0.2	0.7	1.6	8.4
Divorced/separated/widowed	10.0	11.0	19.6	18.5

Source: See Table 3.2.

a. Children who are not a member of one of these groups are included in the totals for all children. This group includes Asian-Americans, Native Americans, and other groups.

children lived with never-married mothers: the range was from 0.1 percent for whites to 1.0 percent for blacks. In 1969 the percentage of children living with never-married mothers was still below 1.0 percent for whites and Hispanics, but was 5.3 percent for black children. Growth of this category accelerated after 1969, and by 1991, 2.6 percent of white, 8.4 percent of Hispanic, and 27.2 percent of black children lived in families headed by never-married women.

The direction of the trend in family structure is similar for whites, blacks, and Hispanics. In all these groups, children are now considerably more likely to live in mother-only families, especially with never-married mothers, than was the case two decades ago.

What impact did these demographic shifts have on the poverty rate? All the demographic groups that have increased in relative size have lower mean incomes and higher poverty rates than the groups that have declined in size. This pattern of change would have raised the aggregate poverty rate even if the rates *within* each of the demographic groups had not changed. Thus, the demographic changes *must* have increased poverty. But by how much? And how do the effects of demographic changes compare with those of changes in the level and distribution of income? The rest of this chapter will be devoted to answering these questions.

Components of Changes in the Poverty Rate

As we have demonstrated, both demographic trends and increasing inequality of incomes have raised the poverty rate in recent decades. While a rising mean income decreases poverty, the mean has grown quite slowly in this period, so this poverty-reducing effect has been much smaller than in the past. To determine the relative importance of economic and demographic factors we rely on a simulation of the trend in poverty.

Economic Factors

To distinguish the effects of changes in the level of income (changes in the mean) from those of changes in the shape of the distribution (changes in inequality), let us first perform a thought experiment. Consider a single demographic group, and suppose that income, adjusted for inflation, grew at the same rate for every family in that group.[2] With this even rate of income growth, the level of inequality would not change: each family's income would rise by the same percentage, and the entire distribution would shift to the right. Because the official poverty line is fixed in real terms, it does not change when real incomes increase. Thus, in this thought experiment, evenly shared economic growth must reduce poverty. The difference between the actual poverty rate and the rate that would result from such even growth is the answer to the question of how much income growth would reduce poverty if inequality remained constant.

The findings from this thought experiment are illustrated in the top panel of Figure 5.1. The dashed curve represents the initial income distribution. Any person living in a family whose income divided by the poverty line is less than 1.0 (to the left of the solid vertical line) is counted as poor. The mean of the distribution is denoted by the dashed vertical line labeled $mean_1$. For this distribution, the proportion of people who are poor is the sum of areas A and B.

The solid curve indicates the income distribution after all incomes have grown at the same rate. The shape of the distribution has not changed, but the mean has increased to $mean_2$ as the entire distribution has shifted to the right. Now only those persons in area B remain poor. The persons in area A have been removed from poverty by economic growth.

Now let us perform another thought experiment, in which we assume that mean income does not change, but that inequality of income increases. That is, the incomes of those at the lower end of the distribution fall while the incomes of those at the top of the distribution rise. The results of this experiment, graphed in the bottom panel of Figure 5.1, indicate what effect rising inequality has on the poverty rate if mean income remains constant.

The solid curve in the bottom panel shows the same income distribution as the solid curve in the top panel, with $mean_2$, and with area B again denoting the poverty population. The dashed curve in the bottom panel shows what the income distribution would be if inequality increased while mean income stayed the same. Increased

Mean increases with inequality constant

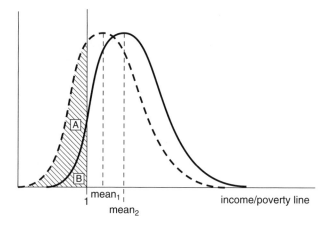

Mean constant with inequality increasing

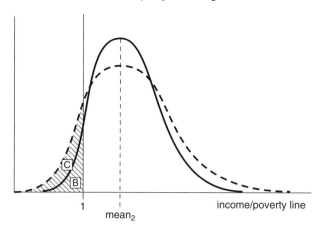

Figure 5.1 Growth and inequality as sources of change in the distribution of income to needs.

inequality with a constant mean raises the poverty rate. The poor are now represented by the sum of areas *B* and *C*; the rise in inequality has moved those in area *C* into poverty.

Combining the two panels in Figure 5.1 illustrates how we distinguish the separate contributions of changes in mean income and changes in inequality to the actual change in poverty between any two years (let us call them Year 1 and Year 2). The actual distribution for any Year 1 is represented by the dashed curve in the top panel with mean$_1$; the actual distribution for any Year 2 by the dashed curve in the bottom panel with mean$_2$.

First we compute the actual rate of increase in mean income from Year 1 to Year 2 and simulate what poverty would have been if every family's income had grown at this same rate. For every individual in our computer file for Year 1, we increase real family income by this same percentage. Then we compare each family's simulated income with the actual poverty line for that family size in Year 2. This simulated income distribution has the same shape (inequality) as that of Year 1, but the mean income of Year 2. Since both distributions have the degree of inequality of Year 1, the difference between the poverty rate for Year 2 associated with this simulated distribution and the actual poverty rate for Year 1 equals the percentage-point change in poverty that is due to the change in the mean. Similarly, the difference between the poverty rate associated with this simulated distribution and the actual rate in Year 2 equals the percentage-point change in poverty that is due to the change in inequality.

Demographic Factors

As we have said, in recent decades the demographic composition of the population has shifted toward groups with above-average rates of poverty. To distinguish the effect of these demographic changes on the overall poverty rate from the effects of the two economic components just discussed, we must perform an additional calculation.

The first step is to calculate what the poverty rate for all persons would have been if our measure of income—adjusted family income divided by the poverty line—had grown at the same rate for everyone while the demographic composition of the population remained constant.[3] We then contrast this simulated poverty rate with a second simulated rate that incorporates the actual demographic changes between Years 1 and 2. The difference between these two simulated rates is the percentage-point change in the poverty rate that is due to demographic changes.[4] By using these two simulated poverty rates and the actual Year 1 and Year 2 rates, we can compute three mutually exclusive components that represent the effects of changes in the mean, demographic changes, and changes in inequality.

To perform this computation for the change in the overall poverty rate between 1973 and 1991, we begin with the actual 1973 observations for each family, then calculate a simulated income distribution based on the assumptions that 1973 demographic composition does not change and that the observed growth in the mean income between 1973 and 1991 is equally shared by all families. This simulation maintains the demographic composition and the inequality of 1973, but has the mean income of 1991. As a result, the difference between this simulated poverty rate and the actual 1973 rate equals the change in the poverty rate that is attributable to income growth.

This first simulation allows us to estimate what every demographic group's 1991 poverty rate would have been if *only* the mean had changed since 1973. We then weight these group-specific poverty rates by the observed 1991 demographic composition of the population. This second simulation incorporates the inequality of 1973, but has the mean *and* the demographic composition of 1991. The difference between the poverty rates from the two simulations equals the percentage-point change in poverty that is accounted for by demographic change. The difference between the poverty rate for all persons from this second simulation and the observed 1991 poverty rate equals the change in poverty that is accounted for by changes in inequality of incomes. By construction, the sum of these three components—the changes attributable to changes in mean income, to demographic changes, and to changes in income inequality—will equal the observed percentage-point change in the poverty rate.

Results of the Simulations

We have performed the calculations described above to investigate changes in the overall poverty rate during the periods 1949–1969 and 1973–1991. As Table 3.4 showed, poverty fell rapidly between 1949 and 1969, from 39.7 percent to 14.4 percent. The official poverty rate reached a historical low in 1973; between that year and 1991 it grew from 10.7 to 12.5 percent.

The Boom Decades

As we showed in Chapter 3, family incomes, adjusted for inflation and declines in family size, more than doubled between 1949 and 1969, and this growth benefited those at all levels of the income distribution. In fact, incomes at the bottom of the distribution rose a bit faster than those at the top.

As a result of the rapid growth in mean adjusted income and the decline in income inequality, the poverty rate fell sharply—by 25.7 percentage points—during this period despite adverse demographic changes (see row 1 of Table 5.3).[5] Row 2a of the table indicates how much poverty would have changed in the twenty-year period

Table 5.3   Decomposition of percentage-point change in the poverty rate for all persons, 1949–1969 and 1973–1991

	1949–1969		1973–1991	
(1) Actual change in poverty rate	−25.7		1.8	
% point change owing to:				
(2) Economic changes	−26.9		−0.1	
(a) Growth in mean adjusted income		−21.4		−2.1
(b) Change in income inequality		−5.5		2.0
(3) Demographic changes	1.2		2.0	
(a) Race/ethnic composition		0.6		0.7
(b) Family structure composition		0.7		1.6
(c) Interaction		−0.1		−0.3

Source: Authors' calculations based on data from Census Bureau computer tapes.
Note: The column entries do not sum exactly to the actual change in row 1 because of rounding.

if the mean of the income distribution had more than doubled, as it actually did (see Table 3.3), but income inequality and the demographic composition of the population had remained exactly as they were in 1949. The size of this hypothetical decline in the poverty rate, 21.4 percentage points, is close to the actual decline shown in row 1; thus most of the large decline in poverty resulted from economic growth.

In fact income did not grow at the same rate for all families, and some of the reduction in poverty resulted from reductions in income inequality; row 2b of the table shows the size of this component: 5.5 percentage points. In other words, in the absence of any demographic changes, the combined impact of growth in mean adjusted incomes and reductions in income inequality would have led to a decline in the poverty rate of 26.9 (21.4 plus 5.5) percentage points, as indicated in row 2 of the table.

The poverty rate for all persons, however, declined by only 25.7 percent (row 1). The difference of 1.2 percentage points, shown in row 3, is total impact of demographic changes. Changes in the racial/ethnic composition of the population (row 3a) and in family structure (row 3b) were of roughly equal importance.[6] Between 1949 and 1969, the impact of demographic changes on the poverty rate was very small relative to that of economic changes.

Slow Growth and Rising Inequality

Rapid economic growth was by far the most important factor accounting for the large reduction in poverty in the two decades following World War II. The situation was very different during the period 1973–1991, which was characterized by slow income growth, rising inequality, and more rapid demographic change.

Until the 1970s, poverty rates consistently rose during recessions and fell during recoveries because the economic expansion during recoveries raised incomes at the bottom of the income distribution as well as at the top. In the 1970s, however, the economy changed in such a way that the link between cyclical recoveries and poverty was severed. The incomes of families at the top of the distribution rose rapidly, while those of families at the bottom either rose slowly or fell. These conditions led to the anomaly of high poverty rates during a period when the average American standard of living reached an all-time high.

The official poverty rate from 1965 to 1991 is graphed in Figure 5.2, using the historical data we have already presented in Chapter 3. Two periods stand out. Before 1973 the poverty rate declined rapidly during expansions, quickly making up the ground lost during recessions, as families across the distribution gained from rapid economic growth. After 1973 average family income continued to increase during economic recoveries, but less dramatically, and the poverty rate never fell back to its 1973 value. As we showed in Table 4.1, median adjusted family income was 10.6 percent higher in 1991 than in 1973. This increase by itself would have lowered poverty if all families had benefited and if there had been no demographic changes. Instead of falling, however, poverty rates rose: despite modest income growth, the official poverty rate was higher in 1991 than it had been in 1973.

The poverty rate has not fallen back to its 1973 level because economic growth has been slow over the past two decades and because demographic changes and rising income inequality have counteracted the modest poverty-reducing effects of this growth. The sec-

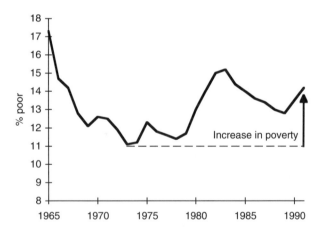

Figure 5.2 Official poverty rate, 1965–1991. (Source: U.S. Bureau of the Census, Current Population Reports, ser. P-60.)

ond column of Table 5.3 presents the results of our calculations of the components of changes in poverty between 1973 and 1991. Our adjusted measure of poverty rose by 1.8 percentage points over this period, from 10.7 to 12.5 percent.

Balanced income growth would have lowered poverty rates by 2.1 points between 1973 and 1991, or about one-tenth of the decline due to income growth over the 1949–1969 period. If there had been no increase in income inequality and no demographic changes, the 1991 poverty rate would have attained an all-time low in 1991—8.6 percent. Even this low rate would have been much higher than Lampman (1971) or Tobin (1967) would have predicted for 1991, because economic growth after 1973 was so much slower than they expected. But it would have been substantially below the rate of 12.7 we calculate for that year. What accounts for the additional 4.1 percentage points?

As indicated in Table 5.3, rising inequality raised the poverty rate by 2.0 percentage points between 1973 and 1991. This increase roughly canceled out the 2.1-point reduction in poverty due to economic growth.[7] Thus increases in inequality just about negated the effect of the 10 percent rise in mean family income over the two decades.

Changes in family structure, primarily a shift away from married-couple families and toward female-headed families, accounted for a 1.6-point increase in the poverty rate, or approximately one-tenth of a percentage point per year.[8] The changing racial and ethnic composition of the population accounted for an additional increase of 0.7 percentage points in the poverty rate, and the total effect of demographic change (including the interaction term) was 2 percentage points. It is important to note that the increase in the number of female-headed families, which is often cited as the primary cause of the rising poverty rate, actually had a smaller effect than the increase in inequality.

Another commonly used way of analyzing the effect on poverty of changes in family structure can be contrasted with our method. It focuses on demographic effects only, leaving economic factors out of the calculation. For example, analysts following this procedure would first note that poverty rose by 1.8 percentage points between

1973 and 1991. Then they would adjust for changes in family structure by applying the 1973 demographic weights to the actual 1991
group-specific poverty rates. They would find that changes in family
structure increased poverty by 1.6 percentage points—a finding that
agrees with ours (see Table 5.3). They would then conclude that
family structure changes accounted for almost all of the increase in
the poverty rate (1.6 of 1.8 percentage points).

Ignoring economic factors leaves this analysis seriously flawed.
Failing to consider the economic factors that led the group-specific
poverty rates to change from their 1973 levels, it takes the 1991
group-specific poverty rates as given, even though those group-
specific rates reflect the actual changes in mean income *and* inequality that occurred between 1973 and 1991.

Our simulation demonstrates that one must explain a 3.9 percentage point increase in poverty, not the 1.8 point observed increase, because, given the actual growth in mean adjusted income,
poverty should have fallen by 2.1 points below the 1973 rate. Thus,
the 1991 group-specific poverty rates are *not* the appropriate basis
for comparison. What must be explained is why poverty in 1991
was 3.9 points above what it would have been had there been no
changes in family structure or inequality.

Our analysis shows that about half of the increase in poverty between 1973 and 1991 was due to rising inequality; about 40 percent
due to changes in family structure. In other words, family structure changes were important, but they were less important than
economic changes. Decompositions that do not attempt to measure
the effects of income growth or changes in inequality erroneously
conclude that economic changes were not important, because, in
the case of the 1973–1991 period, the positive effect of economic
growth just happened to be roughly offset by the negative effect of
rising inequality.

Figure 5.3 summarizes our analysis of the factors contributing to
the changes in the poverty rate during the two historical periods.
There were two major differences between the periods and one similarity. The major difference was the much smaller poverty-reducing
effect of economic growth in the more recent period (−2.1 percentage points, compared with −21.4 points for 1949–1969). The second difference was that changes in inequality had poverty-reducing

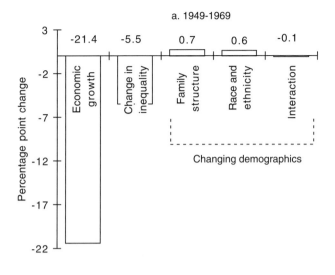

a. 1949-1969

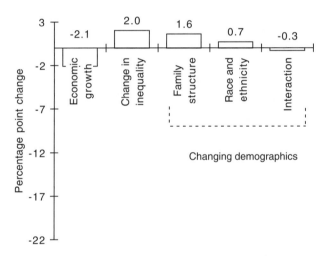

b. 1973-1991

Figure 5.3   Sources of change in the poverty rate. (Source: Authors' calculations from Census Bureau computer tapes.)

effects in the first period (−5.5 percentage points) but shifted to poverty-increasing effects in the second (+2.0 points). The similarity was that in both periods demographic change had a modest poverty-increasing effect: changes in the racial/ethnic composition of the population raised poverty by about 0.7 points during each period. And while changes in family structure were more important in the recent period, their effect on poverty remained smaller than that of rising inequality.

If the analysis summarized in Table 5.3 is restricted to children, the results differ somewhat for the recent period because changes in family structure have been greater for children than for the population as a whole. The child poverty rate, as we measure it, rose by 5.7 percentage points between 1973 and 1991. Had there been no change in the living arrangements of children or in income inequality, economic growth during that period would have *decreased* children's poverty rate by 1.3 percentage points. We find that changes in family structure accounted for about two-thirds (4.6 percentage points) of the total increase in child poverty, and that rising inequality among families with children accounted for about one-third (2.2 points) of the total increase.

Thus for children, in contrast to the population as a whole, changes in family structure did more to increase poverty than did rising inequality. For both children and the overall population, however, the most important difference between the boom decades after World War II and the more recent period was the slow economic growth after 1973. Increases in mean income reduced poverty among children by 27 percentage points between 1949 and 1969 but by only 1.3 points between 1973 and 1991.

Sources of Increased Inequality

While changes in the shape of the income distribution reduced poverty by 5.5 percentage points between 1949 and 1969, they *increased* poverty by 2.0 points between 1973 and 1991. To investigate the sources of this increased inequality of family income, we disaggregate a standard measure of inequality, the coefficient of variation squared, into three components: one related to changes in the distribution of the earnings of family heads, one related to changes in the distribution of the earnings of other family members, and a third associated with changes in the distribution of all other sources of income.[9]

Figure 5.4 shows the results of applying this calculation to the co-efficient of variation squared of adjusted family income divided by the poverty line for persons living in families headed by nonelderly men.[10] The results are similar to those obtained using the other measures of inequality discussed in Chapter 3: inequality decreased between 1949 and 1969 and increased between 1973 and 1991.

In the earlier period, decreasing inequality in two components of family income—earnings of male family heads and earnings of other family members—accounted for all of the reduction in income inequality. In the later period, although changes in the earnings of other family members (primarily wives) continued to have an

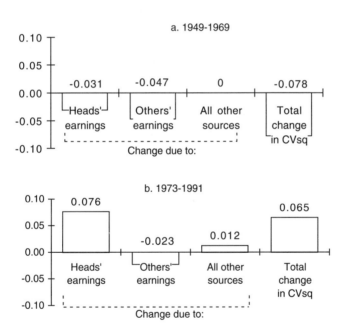

Figure 5.4 Sources of change in coefficient of variation squared, persons living in families headed by nonelderly males. (Source: Authors' calculations from Census Bureau computer tapes.)

inequality-reducing effect, inequality in family income nonetheless increased because of a substantial increase in inequality of men's earnings. Changes in men's earnings caused the coefficient of variation squared to rise by 0.076, more than the total increase of 0.065.[11] Increased inequality in income from other sources (property income and government cash transfers) had a modest inequality-increasing effect. Thus changes in labor markets were the primary source of the rising inequality of family income after 1973, which in turn was an important factor contributing to the increase in poverty.

To reiterate the points made in this chapter, we find, as other researchers have, that demographic changes, particularly the shift toward more female-headed families, contributed to the high poverty rates of recent years. Changes in family structure raised the poverty rate by 1.6 percentage points over an eighteen-year period, or by roughly 0.1 percentage points per year.

Economic changes, however, were even more important. The slow economic growth from the 1970s to the 1990s was only enough to decrease poverty by about 0.16 points per year. Meanwhile, the poverty-reducing effect of this growth was offset by increased inequality of family income, which had a stronger poverty-increasing effect than did changes in family structure. Our findings strongly point to the importance of changes in labor markets, especially the slow growth and increased inequality of men's earnings.

Chapter 6

Changes in Labor Markets

While all components of family income (earnings, property income, public transfers) grew more slowly and less equally after 1973 than before, the component that diverged most from post–World War II trends, and that contributed most to the rising inequality of family incomes in the period 1973–1991, was labor market earnings of men. That the distribution of earnings for men became more unequal is now uncontested. There was some debate in the late 1970s and early 1980s about whether the increased inequality reflected structural, long-term changes in labor markets or was a short-term phenomenon due to recessions. Continued increases in earnings inequality during the long expansion of the 1980s, however, converted even the sternest skeptics.

Having reached agreement on *what* had happened, analysts began tracking down possible explanations for *why* it had happened. Many explanations that seemed plausible at first were ruled out in the course of their investigations. For example, reductions in work effort brought on by growing government transfers could not have played a major role, because labor market groups with little or no access to public transfers, such as full-time, full-year workers, also experienced large increases in inequality. Furthermore, earnings inequality for all men continued to grow even after reductions in unemployment insurance and welfare were implemented in the early 1980s.

Other explanations remain prime suspects. One is that the increased inequality was largely driven by technological change.

In recent years important technological and organizational innovations have changed the way businesses are organized and operated. For example, the advent of ever-faster computers introduced robotics into manufacturing and transformed the delivery of some business services, such as accounting. These new technologies raised the demand for highly skilled workers relative to those with lower skills. As a result, the wages of the former group increased, while the latter group faced declining wages and diminished employment opportunities.

Another possible explanation for the increased inequality is the major deindustrialization of the U.S. economy over the past twenty-five years, which shifted workers out of manufacturing and into the service sector. For example, some blue-collar workers from higher-paying manufacturing industries lost their jobs and could only find new ones in lower-paying service industries. The decrease in their wages drove a wedge between them and the more fortunate blue-collar workers who did not lose their manufacturing jobs. Deindustrialization may also have increased the earnings gap between blue-collar and white-collar workers: the demand for managers and other more highly trained workers may have increased in both manufacturing industries and the emerging high-tech service industries, which pay higher wages than other parts of the service sector.

No single change in the structure of labor markets explains all or even most of the changes in the level and distribution of earnings. None stands out as the "smoking gun." In the next chapter, therefore, we will explore several possible explanations.

In this chapter we will review evidence on the slow growth in earnings and increased earnings inequality. We will also review evidence on earnings mobility, that is, the extent to which workers move up or down in the earnings distribution. Rising mobility might decrease the importance of rising inequality. For example, if wages in low-skill jobs declined, but people stayed in these jobs for shorter periods and then moved to better jobs, the effects of the increases in wage inequality might be offset by the effects of increases in mobility. If this were the case, rising inequality would be of less concern to policymakers. The evidence, however, points to little or no change in mobility in recent years. Workers at the bottom of the distribution earned less, and had no better chance of leaving the bottom, in the early 1990s than in the early 1970s.

Changes in the Level of Earnings

The increase in inequality has been pervasive. Wages of workers at the top of the earnings distribution were substantially higher in the 1980s than in the 1970s.[1] At the other end of the distribution, wages (adjusted for inflation) actually declined. These conclusions are derived from many studies (reviewed in Levy and Murnane, 1992), which typically analyze earnings data from the annual CPS or the decennial censuses.

Figure 6.1 shows the trend in median weekly wage and salary income for men and women (including part-time and part-year workers, but excluding nonworkers) from 1963 to 1992.[2] Average earnings grew steadily from 1963 to 1973, but stopped growing in 1973 as productivity growth slowed. Men's median weekly earnings increased by 24 percent between 1963 and 1973, then began a

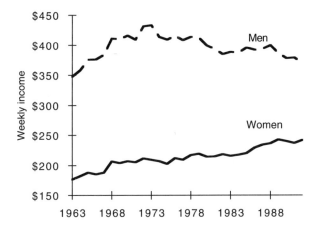

Figure 6.1   Median weekly wage and salary income for men and women, 1963–1992. Wages in 1986 dollars using the CPI-X. Includes part-time and part-year workers with positive earnings. (Source: Update of Karoly, 1993, table 2B2.)

steady decline; in 1989, the last business cycle peak, they were still 11 percent lower than in 1973.[3]

The pattern for women is different: their real earnings increased by 18 percent between 1963 and 1973, and by an additional 16 percent between 1973 and 1989. Because women who entered the labor market in the late 1980s worked more and received higher wages, on average, than those who entered in the early 1960s, part of this increase reflects a change in the composition of the female labor force. Nonetheless, the continued growth of women's earnings after 1973 is in stark contrast to the decline of men's earnings over this period.

The gender gap among all workers has declined over the past two decades. The ratio of women's median wages to men's hovered around 0.5 before 1973, then started to increase, reaching 0.6 by 1989 and 0.65 by 1992. The ratio for full-time, full-year workers rose almost as much (from about 0.6 to about 0.7) over this period, indicating that women's wage rates as well as their hours worked continued to increase after 1973. Thus, while earnings have grown slowly on average and earnings inequality has increased, inequality between men and women has declined.

Changes in the Distribution of Earnings

Between 1963 and 1973, earnings increased slightly for men at all points in the earnings distribution. The real weekly wages of men at the 90th percentile rose by 27 percent, while those of men at the 10th percentile grew by 16 percent.[4] While growth was higher for the highest-paid men, low-wage and middle-wage workers also experienced increases. Over this decade the weekly wages of women at the 90th and 10th percentiles grew by 22 percent and 41 percent, respectively. Thus inequality increased for men but fell for women.

The watershed year for men is 1979, when the real weekly earnings of men at the 10th percentile began to fall. In 1983 they reached a low of $99, the same level as in 1963; in 1989 they were 10 percent lower than in 1979 and 16 percent lower than in 1973; and after the recession of the early 1990s they were back down to the 1963 level. In contrast, the real earnings of men at the top of the distribution rose substantially: by 1989 those of men at the 90th percentile were 7 percent higher than in 1979 and 35 percent higher than in 1963.

For women at the 10th percentile, real weekly earnings grew by 7 percent between 1979 and 1989.[5] Even during the recession of the early 1990s their earnings grew by another 2 percent. Women at the 90th percentile did even better, with their earnings growing by 25 percent between 1979 and 1992.

Figure 6.2 shows a commonly used summary measure of earnings inequality, the ratio of the earnings of workers at the 90th percentile to those of workers at the 10th percentile. For example, the ratio of 7.5 for women in 1978 indicates that a woman at the 90th percentile earned seven and a half times as much as a woman at the 10th percentile. Thus the lower the 90/10 ratio, the more equal the earnings distribution. The earnings of women became more equal between 1963 and the late 1970s, then became considerably less so after the recession of the early 1980s before plateauing at a level comparable to the early 1970s.

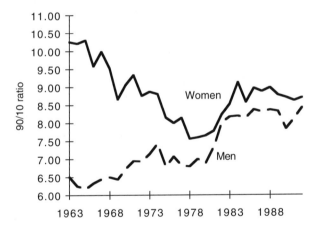

Figure 6.2   Ratio of weekly wage and salary income for workers at 90th percentile to workers at 10th percentile, by sex, 1963–1992. Includes part-time and part-year workers with positive earnings. (Source: Update of Karoly, 1993, table 2B2.)

In contrast, inequality of men's weekly earnings began increasing in the late 1960s and continued to rise through the mid-1980s.[6] Inequality of annual earnings increased as well. The largest increase came during the 1981–1982 recession, which exacted a severe toll on less-skilled male workers but largely bypassed high-earning men. As a result, the 90/10 ratio increased from 6.88 to 8.48 between 1980 and 1992.

Since the mid-1980s the trend in inequality of earnings has stabilized. As Figure 6.2 shows, the 90/10 ratios for both women and men were about the same in the early 1990s as in the mid-1980s. What is striking is that inequality has plateaued at a very high level and shows no signs of falling, in spite of the long Reagan recovery and the Clinton recovery of the mid-1990s. At most, the trend toward greater inequality has stalled.

Changes in Inequality between Groups

Earnings inequality can be divided into two components. The first is inequality *between* groups, which compares the average earnings of workers at different levels of educational attainment or years of work experience. The second is inequality *within* groups, which focuses on differences in earnings among workers at the same level of education or experience. Both components affect total inequality. We will focus on between-group inequality in this section and on within-group inequality in the next.

A common measure of inequality between educational groups is the returns to a college degree, that is, the ratio of the average earnings of workers with a college education to those of workers with only a high school education. While college graduates have always received higher average earnings than high school graduates, the premium received for the extra four years of education has varied dramatically over time.

For simplicity, we will compare workers with under ten years of experience (young workers) with those with thirty to thirty-nine years of experience (older workers).[7] Among young men in 1979, college graduates earned 23 percent more than high school graduates; that is, at this level of experience the premium for a college education was 23 percent. By 1989 it was 43 percent. The college premium also rose for older male workers, from 42 percent in 1979 to 65 percent in 1989. For women it grew even more: from 32 to 54 percent for the younger group and from 36 to 70 percent for the older group.

The rising relative earnings of college graduates can be partially explained by changes in their relative supply. The college-educated proportion of the workforce grew more slowly in the 1980s than in the 1970s, while the demand for college-educated workers steadily increased. As demand rose faster than supply, average real wages for male college graduates rose by about 8 percent, while wages for male high school graduates fell by 40 percent (see Katz and Murphy, 1992).

Earnings differentials between workers at different levels of experience (with educational attainment held constant) also increased. Male high school graduates with 30–39 years of experience earned 60 percent more than those with less than ten years of experience in 1979, and 75 percent more by 1989. Similar patterns emerged for male college graduates and for women in both educational categories. Katz and Murphy (1992) show that this continued an upward trend in returns to experience dating back at least to the 1960s, a trend that peaked in the mid-1980s.

The rising premiums for college and for experience led to a dramatic decline in the relative wages of young high school graduates. Juhn, Murphy, and Pierce (1993) illustrate this decline by noting that real wages for young high school graduates at the 10th percentile were roughly 18 percent lower in the late 1980s than in 1963. Thus one reason poverty has not fallen and inequality has risen is that the earnings of the least-skilled workers have been rapidly falling behind those of other workers for almost two decades.

Changes in Inequality within Groups

Inequality also increased among persons with the same levels of experience and education. Between-group inequality and within-group inequality grew at roughly the same rates (see Levy and Murnane, 1992).[8]

The increased inequality of wages among workers with the same characteristics exacerbated economic hardship for the least-skilled and least-experienced workers. Some young high school dropouts lost ground not only to high school and college graduates but also to other high school dropouts. Katz and Murphy find large increases in the 90/10 ratio for persons of the same gender, experience, and education. For men, the ratio was 1.90 in 1969—that is, among those with the same education and experience, men at the 90th percentile earned roughly 90 percent more than men at the 10th percentile. By 1987 this measure of within-group inequality had risen to roughly 2.20.

The wage differential between the 90th and 10th percentiles increased for both young and older workers and for both high school and college graduates. In all cases, real wages grew modestly for those in the upper percentiles but grew only slightly or, more often, declined for those in the lower percentiles. It is widely recognized that young workers with little education who worked in manufacturing lost ground during the 1980s. Less well known is the fact that inequality also increased among highly educated workers and within almost every industry. The problem was much deeper than the decay of the rust belt or job flight from the inner cities. What the United States experienced during the 1980s was akin to a disease that affected all parts of the body.

International Comparisons

Table 6.1 presents changes in the 90/10 ratio for male workers in seven industrialized countries.[9] In the United States in 1979, for example, the 90/10 ratio was 3.85: that is, full-time workers at the 90th percentile earned $3.85 for every dollar earned by those at the 10th percentile. By 1986 this had increased to $4.60. In all seven countries, inequality of earnings increased during the periods covered in the table. This pattern is confirmed by country-specific studies which show that earnings inequality also increased in Australia, Canada, and Japan, and to a lesser extent in France and Sweden. The only European countries without such an increase were Italy and Germany. While there is a wide disparity in the size of the increases, the rise in inequality was by no means unique to the United States.

In these other countries, too, inequality increased both between

Table 6.1 Changes in inequality of earnings in seven industrialized countries during the mid-1980s

	90/10 ratio		
	Initial year	Final year	Annual change
Full-time workers			
Australia (1981–1985)	2.52	2.66	1.4%
Netherlands (1983–1987)	2.33	2.46	1.4
Sweden (1981–1987)	2.11	2.19	0.7
United Kingdom (1979–1986)	2.53	3.01	2.7
United States (1979–1986)	3.85	4.58	2.7
All workers			
Canada (1981–1987)	3.90	4.81	3.9
France (1979–1984)	3.07	3.45	2.5
United States (1979–1986)	4.29	5.82	5.1

Source: Gottschalk and Joyce (1992); data from the Luxembourg Income Study.

groups and within groups. The experience premium between young and old workers widened, and in many countries, returns to education also increased, although much less than they did in the United States.

Gottschalk and Joyce (1992) show that the rise in inequality in the seven countries resulted from both an increase in the earnings of those at the top of the distribution and a decline in the earnings of those at the bottom. Furthermore, with few exceptions, the lower the decile of workers, the larger the decline (or the smaller the growth) in their earnings. The United States differs from these other countries primarily in the size of the increase in inequality, with only the United Kingdom experiencing increases of similar magnitude.

Countries with more centralized labor markets either escaped the increases (Germany and Italy) or experienced relatively mild ones (for example, the Scandinavian countries). The fact that wage rates in these countries are largely set by coordinated or centralized bargaining between associations of employers and employees means that, at least for a while, wages could diverge from market forces (see Freeman, 1994). If the social consensus in a country is that increased inequality is unacceptable, and if a country either can train less-skilled workers to fill the high-demand jobs or is willing to accept increased unemployment for less-skilled workers, then it is possible to restrain rising wage inequality. The fact that the slow increase in inequality accelerated in the 1990s in some of these countries (Gottschalk, Gustafsson, and Palmer, 1994) suggests that there may not be a political will to continue to use these institutions to moderate market forces.

Many countries either could not or did not interfere directly in the labor market to prevent the increase in inequality. This, however, did not mean that they allowed rising inequality of earnings to translate into a rise in inequality of family incomes. As Gottschalk (1994), Hanratty and Blank (1992), and others have shown, most countries offset some of the impact of the rise in labor market inequality by either increasing transfers or decreasing taxes for families at the bottom of the income distribution. The United States stands out in its failure to undertake sufficient changes in tax or transfer policies to offset the increase in earnings inequality. As a result, in the United States the rising wage inequality translated into rising inequality of family incomes.

Changes in Earnings Mobility

In response to the mounting evidence that economic rewards were being distributed less equally, some conservative analysts sought to shift the focus in policy discussions away from increased inequality toward earnings mobility.[10] They maintained that even if the gaps between earnings at different positions increased, the workers occupying those positions might have become more economically mobile. In such a case, increased inequality in one year might be the cost of greater economic opportunity in the long run for those who started at the bottom of the distribution.

Mobility and inequality are closely related but conceptually distinct concepts. Inequality measures the dispersion of earnings in any year. Mobility measures movements across the earnings distribution over time. If mobility is high, then people with low earnings in one year are likely to have higher earnings in a subsequent year. Similarly, higher earners have a substantial chance of losing their advantaged position. The higher the mobility, the greater the likelihood that people will move throughout the distribution so that few people will remain permanently rich or poor.[11]

Inequality and mobility are separate and distinct attributes of a society. For example, a very equal society might have low mobility, in which case each individual might be in an unchanging income class but income differences across classes would be small. Alternatively, a very unequal society might have high mobility, in which case the poor would have very low incomes and the rich would have very high incomes but no one would remain poor or rich for very long.

Inequality can be thought of as analogous to a hotel with rooms of very different quality.[12] Some rooms are luxurious, while others are spartan. The hotel guests, therefore, have very unequal accommodations. Economic mobility is akin to movement between rooms. If guests are not permitted to change from one room to another, then they are immobile. But if guests move randomly from room to room each night, then those in the best rooms on any night are as likely as those in the worst rooms on that night to find themselves in the undesirable rooms the following night. In this case the distribution of rooms is still unequal, but mobility is high.

This example can be expanded to clarify the differences among the effects of growth in mean earnings, changes in earnings inequality, and changes in earnings mobility. Balanced economic growth is akin to upgrading all hotel rooms to the same extent. If nothing else changes, there will still be better and worse rooms and the level of inequality will remain the same.[13] Everyone's room will be more attractive than it used to be, but if everyone stays in the same room there will still be no mobility. (In terms of the income distribution, the mean of the distribution rises but the correlation of incomes across time periods does not change.) If some of the furniture from the spartan rooms is removed and used to make the better rooms even more luxurious, inequality will increase. Mobility changes only when the rate at which people move from room to room changes.

The absolute well-being of the occupants is affected by three possible changes—upgrading the furnishings of all rooms (growth), reshuffling furniture among rooms (changes in inequality), or reshuffling people among rooms (mobility). If we consider persons living in sparsely furnished rooms to be poor, then they may escape poverty if furniture is added to all rooms (growth), if furniture is reallocated to their rooms (changes in inequality), or if they move to better rooms (mobility).

There is considerable evidence (reviewed in Atkinson, Bourguignon, and Morrison, 1992) of substantial mobility throughout the earnings distribution. People who start at the bottom of the distribution often move to higher levels.

Moffitt and Gottschalk (1993) ranked persons according to their earnings in one year and tracked their mobility across the earnings distribution in the following year. They found that fully 67 percent of persons in the lowest quintile of the earnings distribution in one year remained in that quintile in the following year. Of the remaining 33 percent, most moved up to the second-lowest quintile. Only 8 percent moved up to the middle quintile, and a very small number made it to the top quintile (see Table 6.2, row 1).

Workers who began at the top of the distribution had similar patterns of mobility. About 69 percent of those in the highest quintile remained at the top; most of the rest fell into the second-

Table 6.2   One-year quintile mobility rates for log annual earnings

		Quintile distribution at t				
Quintile at $t - 1$	Sum	Bottom quintile	Next-to-bottom quintile	Middle quintile	Next-to-top quintile	Top quintile
Bottom quintile	100	67	21	8	3	1
Next-to-bottom quintile	100	20	49	22	7	2
Middle quintile	100	7	21	44	22	6
Next-to-top quintile	100	4	7	20	47	22
Top quintile	100	2	3	7	20	69

Source: Moffitt and Gottschalk (1993). Mobility rates are measured over the period 1969 to 1987 for white males aged 20 to 59.

highest quintile; and only 12 percent fell into the middle or lower quintiles.[14]

This evidence that the United States exhibits substantial mobility does not imply that mobility has increased. One way of measuring *changes* in mobility is to calculate the probability that a person stays in the same quintile in two different years. If the probability declines, mobility has increased. Moffitt and Gottschalk (1993) find that there is no evidence that earnings mobility increased during the 1980s. Hungerford (1993) and Gottschalk, McLanahan, and Sandefur (1994) show that income mobility also did not change in recent years. In every year, roughly 80 percent of persons in the lowest quartile remained in the bottom quartile in the following year.[15]

For the past two decades, the labor market has been characterized by slow earnings growth and rising inequality in earnings, especially for men. Because earnings mobility has not changed very much, the prospects of the least-skilled workers have diminished. Our task now is to explore the potential causes for this disappointing economic performance.

Chapter 7

Why Inequality of Earnings Increased

There are good reasons to try to understand how fundamental changes in the economy contributed to the changes in the distribution of wages. If we understood the causal mechanisms, we could predict whether inequality would continue to increase or whether it would return to the level of the 1970s. For example, if we knew that inequality had increased primarily because of demographic changes, such as the entrance of the large baby-boom generation into the labor market, then it would be easy to predict how further changes in the size of the labor force would affect inequality. Since the next generation of workers has already been born, we can estimate the size of future labor market cohorts with some accuracy.[1] Likewise, if the rise in the returns to college education resulted from a temporary shortage of college graduates, then we would expect the higher returns to education to induce a potentially self-correcting increase in college enrollments.

An understanding of the causes of the slow growth and increased inequality of earnings can also inform public policy. If the increase in inequality is not likely to reverse itself, then government interventions will be needed to offset its effects. For example, if the shift of jobs away from the manufacturing sector is a primary cause of the rise in inequality, then policymakers may want to consider policies to offset the consequences of that industrial shift. Or, if the dislocation of workers from manufacturing causes only temporary earnings losses, then the appropriate policy may be to subsidize low-income people who fall on temporary hard times.

While the increase in earnings inequality is well documented, much less is known about its causes. Theories abound. Some authors have speculated that inequality increased because of supply-side changes in the labor market, such as the entrance of the baby-boom generation beginning in the early 1970s. According to this view, the inflow of new workers depressed entry-level wages and the wages of less-educated older workers who had to compete with the new entrants for low-skill jobs.

Others have focused on the demand side, stressing, among other factors, the decline of the manufacturing sector and the globalization of labor and capital markets. As these analysts see it, increased international competition caused a decline in industrial production in the United States. The economy lost "good jobs" that could be performed by workers with little formal education. International competition also weakened unions, which have traditionally raised average wages of blue-collar workers and narrowed discrepancies among union members. According to this argument, the decline of the rust belt and the expansion of service-sector jobs led to lower wages for semiskilled workers who went from the assembly line to the fast food counter. In contrast, those with higher skills benefited as globalization increased demand for workers in the financial and high-technology sectors.

Other analysts have stressed the importance of changes in public policies, such as the restriction of benefits and eligibility in social welfare programs and the decline in the inflation-adjusted minimum wage. According to this view, an unintended effect of these policies was to weaken the work effort of the least-skilled.

No consensus has been reached on which of these factors, if any, best explains the increase in inequality. Researchers have narrowed the range of possible explanations by identifying theories that are not consistent with the data or that can account for only a small portion of the increase. Some progress has been made in eliminating hypotheses that are grossly inconsistent with the facts, but several competing theories are still viable.

It is also possible that change in the distribution of earnings is the norm, and that the increase in inequality that began in the late 1960s and accelerated during the 1980s is not an aberration. Perhaps the modest leveling of inequality during the postwar boom was the anomaly. A look at economic theory and history suggests that change, not stability, may be the norm.

Economic Theory and Historical Evidence

Students of economics are taught that, in a market economy, competition leads to an efficient allocation of resources and encourages technological innovation, but that economic efficiency and equity sometimes conflict.[2] There is nothing about a market economy that ensures that a rising standard of living will be accompanied by reduced inequality. For example, technological change may bid up the price of factors that were already in scarce supply and thus already commanding high prices. If the scarce factor in question is college-educated workers, the normal functioning of an efficiently changing market will raise their already high wages even higher.

Wages tend to rise whenever demand for a certain type of labor exceeds its supply. Markets make no distinction between "haves" and "have-nots." If the introduction of a new technology, such as computerization, leads firms to increase their demand for managers and reduce their demand for typists, then the wages of already lower-paid secretaries will fall and the wages of the higher-paid managers will rise.

The magnitude of the changes in wages will depend on firms' ability to adjust their hiring decisions in response to wage levels and on workers' ability to change occupations. For example, if a firm's production process requires a fixed number of managers, then higher wages for managers will not decrease the firm's demand for them. Likewise, if the new higher wages paid to managers do not induce an inflow of workers from other occupations into this one, then again the wages of managers will increase. The wages of workers who are already highly paid will continue to rise until they become so high that firms cut back their demand for managers or that other workers move into this occupation and create the supply needed to match the increased demand.

Likewise, secretaries' wages will decline until they are so low that firms decide to start rehiring secretaries, or so low that secretaries decide to leave this occupation, thus reducing their supply to match the lower demand. The result may be a decline in the wages of those who are already paid relatively little, and a rise in the pay of the already affluent.

In summary, economic theory predicts neither that a market economy will yield an equitable distribution of earnings nor that the distribution will be stable over time. Market forces may lead to the type of increases in inequality the U.S. economy has experienced in recent decades; they may also lead to an opposite trend toward greater equality.[3]

There is ample historical evidence that changes in earnings inequality are the rule, not the exception. Williamson and Lindert (1980) document a sharp increase in inequality in the second half of the 1800s, which they label the "antebellum surge." Inequality stayed high into the twentieth century, declined during World War I, and regained its antebellum high by the eve of the Great Depression. The Depression, however, was a great leveler, bringing decreases in inequality that continued through what Goldin and Margo (1992) call the "great contraction" of the 1940s. In 1940 white men at the 90th percentile earned $4.11 for every $1.00 earned by white men at the 10th percentile of the earnings distribution. By 1950 this 90/10 ratio had dropped to $2.88. The very low unemployment rates during the war and the wage controls imposed by the price stabilization board were partly responsible for this narrowing of the wage gap. The narrowing continued well after the war, however, and reflected a substantial drop in the returns to education as the supply of college-educated workers, partly because of the GI bill, expanded much faster than the demand for their skills.

In sum, neither economic theory nor economic history suggests that a market economy should lead to a stable distribution of earnings. Prices adjust to equate supply with demand. When demand for skilled workers outstrips supply, the wages of those at the top of the distribution pull apart from those at the bottom, unless institutional factors such as labor unions or government policies offset the effects of these market forces.

Alternative Explanations

The hypotheses that have been suggested to explain the increased inequality of wages during the 1980s can be classified into four broad groups. Hypotheses in the first group focus on institutional changes that may have affected wages, such as changes in the minimum wage and in tax laws. Those in the second focus on changes that may have affected labor supply, such as the entry of large cohorts into the labor market. The third group focuses primarily on changes in demand, such as may arise when globalization of markets leads to a decline in manufacturing or when the introduction of new technologies reduces the demand for less-educated workers. The fourth type of hypothesis attributes the increase in inequality to increased instability of earnings. This taxonomy is a useful organizing device, but it is important to recognize that these are not four mutually exclusive sets of hypotheses. Several factors could have been operating at the same time to cause inequality to rise.

Two broad conclusions emerge from the recent literature by labor economists. First, no single cause had an effect that was large enough to account for the observed increase in wage and earnings inequality. Several potential causes can be rejected, but many are consistent with the trends in the data. Second, only demand-side factors can explain why employment of skilled workers increased at the same time that firms had to pay them higher wages. Supply-side hypotheses cannot explain why employers hired more skilled workers even though their costs to the firm had increased.

Wage-Setting Institutions

The Minimum Wage. Between 1981 and April 1990 the minimum wage was fixed in nominal terms at $3.35 per hour. Because of rising inflation, however, its real value declined by 44 percent during this period. Meanwhile, average wages increased modestly. As a result, the minimum wage fell from 46 percent of the average wage in 1981 to 35 percent in 1989.

Figure 7.1 plots trends between 1963 and 1991 in the inflation-adjusted minimum wage (in 1991 dollars) and the 90/10 ratio for weekly wages for all men with earnings. The occasional adjustments of the minimum wage in the 1960s and 1970s tended to keep pace with inflation: between 1963 and 1978 the minimum wage was typically about $5.50 in 1991 dollars. This pattern, however, was

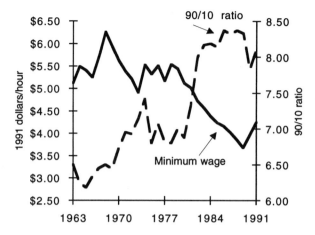

Figure 7.1 Inflation-adjusted minimum wage and 90/10 ratio for men's weekly wages, 1963–1991. (Source: Minimum wage data in 1991 dollars from the 1993 *Statistical Abstract of the United States.*)

reversed after 1978. The real value of the minimum wage steadily eroded from that year until 1990, when the nominal minimum wage was increased to $4.25 per hour. Despite increases, the real minimum wage in the early 1990s was well below that of the 1970s. This erosion may have been partially responsible for the increase in inequality of earnings during the 1980s.

The falling real value of the minimum wage cannot explain much of the increase, however, because inequality rose in almost all education and experience groups. While the minimum wage may account for a significant amount of the economic hardship experienced by young people and workers with low education, it cannot account for much of the increase in inequality among prime-age college graduates.

Horrigan and Mincy (1993) simulated the effect on inequality of indexing the minimum wage to the inflation rate.[4] They found that such a policy would have only a modest effect on earnings inequality. In 1987, for example, male workers in the two lowest quintiles received 12.28 percent of aggregate earnings; if the minimum wage had been indexed for inflation, they would have received 12.45 percent. The effect on inequality of family income would be even smaller, since many of the low-earnings workers who may receive the minimum wage are teenagers who live in high-income families.

Declines in Union Membership.   Whether unions tend to increase or decrease inequality depends on several factors, some of which offset each other. On the one hand, unions raise the wages of their members relative to those of workers who are not covered by union contracts, thus tending to increase inequality among workers of similar characteristics. On the other hand, if the wages of unionized workers are lower than the average wages of all workers (including those with higher levels of education and other income-enhancing characteristics), then unions will tend to decrease inequality by bringing their members closer to the overall average. Finally, unions tend to decrease inequality in unionized firms by reallocating payments within the firm to lower-income workers. Which of these forces dominates is an empirical question that has been addressed in a large body of research: the evidence indicates that unions do more to equalize earnings than to make them less equal. (See Freeman, 1993, for a review of this evidence.) Therefore, inequality should be higher when a smaller portion of the labor force is covered by union contracts.

The proportion of the workforce that is unionized has been falling since the 1950s, but the pace of deunionization accelerated dramatically after 1975. About 29 percent of the workforce was unionized in 1975, but by 1991 this figure had dropped to about 18 percent. If unions are an equalizing force, this decline in their membership may account for part of the rise in inequality. Freeman (1993) has calculated that reductions in unionization can account for roughly 20 percent of the increase in earnings inequality since the 1970s.[5] "Overall," he concludes, "declining unionization was a supporting player in the story of the increase in inequality: Rosencrantz or Guildenstern, not Hamlet" (p. 159).

It is not surprising that deunionization accounts for only a portion of the increase in inequality, since earnings became less equally distributed within almost all groups of workers, including many only tangentially affected by unions. Furthermore, union membership also declined in the 1970s, when the earnings of high school graduates were still increasing relative to those of college graduates. The fact that the workers most likely to benefit from unionization were gaining even as union membership fell indicates that other factors were also affecting earnings inequality and were important enough to offset the effects of declines in union power.

Changes in Income Tax Laws.   Another possible explanation of the increase in inequality has to do with changes in taxation of the wealthy. Feenberg and Poterba (1992) point out that reductions in marginal tax rates reduced the incentive for the wealthy to shelter income after 1986. Instead of taking compensation in the form of stock options or deferred compensation, they were more likely to receive higher salaries or dividends.

Because the change in marginal tax rates did not take effect immediately, there was a strong incentive to defer receiving taxable wages until the change took effect. For people in the highest tax bracket, an extra dollar of income reported in 1986 was worth only $0.50 in after-tax dollars, but if that dollar was deferred until January 1988 it would yield $0.72 after taxes. This change in the law encouraged the wealthy to lower their 1986 income by deferring income until 1988. The resulting increase in reported incomes for high-income people would not necessarily reflect an increase in actual income, but would lead to increases in measured inequality.

Feenberg and Poterba find that much of the increase in reported incomes of the wealthy did occur during the period affected by the change in the tax law and was concentrated among a very small group of taxpayers. Therefore, changes in the tax law may have been responsible for some of the changes in reported income at the top of the income distribution.

This argument is plausible, but several caveats are in order. First, it is based on circumstantial evidence. Many other economic changes occurred during these years and could have affected the reported income of wealthy taxpayers. These include changes in the earnings of high-skilled workers, changing returns to property, and changing patterns of investment. Second, at best this argument explains a one-time increase in measured inequality, but, as we have shown, inequality rose over a much longer period. Finally, at best, this argument applies only to the wealthiest persons—those few who receive compensation in a form that is easily deferred across tax years. Because inequality increased in other years and for high earners who were unaffected by changes in the tax law, other important forces had to be affecting the earnings distribution.

Supply-Side Factors

Cohort Size. During the 1970s there was a large increase in the number of young workers and wives entering the labor force for the first time. The labor force increased by 1.7 percent per year in the 1960s, by 2.6 percent in the 1970s, and again by 1.6 percent in the 1980s. The substantial inflow of less-experienced workers into the labor market during the same period when inequality began to increase led some analysts to suggest that changes in labor supply were the primary causal factor.

It is plausible that demographic phenomena could have caused the changes in the earnings distribution. The increase in job seekers as the baby-boom generation entered the labor force could have led to lower wages for inexperienced workers. Even if this labor supply effect on wage rates was modest, the influx of young workers would still have increased inequality because inequality within age groups tends to be highest for the young.

The effect on the distribution of earnings would have been stronger if the surge in labor supply *did* depress entry-level wages. Competition from new entrants for a limited number of jobs would put downward pressure on wages for these jobs. This decrease in wage levels, coupled with the increased proportion of the workforce receiving entry-level wages, would have further increased between-group inequality.

A demographic explanation, however, cannot account for the continued increase in inequality during the 1980s. If the rapid growth of the labor force in the 1970s increased inequality, then the slower growth of the 1980s should have caused a decline in inequality. There were fewer new entrants in the 1980s, so there was less downward pressure on entry-level wages from the supply side. Inequality continued to increase during the 1980s, both between groups and within groups, and the dearth of young workers did not lead to a closing of the gap between young and older workers. Thus other factors must have been important in the 1980s.

Immigration. Immigration, like the baby boom, increases the relative supply of less-skilled workers, and thus could partially explain the decline in the wages of less-skilled workers. In order to judge its importance, it is necessary to calculate the impact of legal plus illegal immigration on the relative numbers of workers at different levels of educational attainment.

Borjas, Freeman, and Katz (1992) find that legal and illegal immigrants are much more likely to be high school dropouts and less likely to be college graduates than the rest of the U.S. workforce. Thus, since the late 1970s, immigration substantially raised the relative number of less-skilled workers and should have put downward pressure on their wages. Borjas, Freeman, and Katz do not separate the impact of immigration from the impact of international trade. They estimate that roughly one-third of the increase in the premium to education may be due to these two factors, with immigration being the more important.

While increases in immigration are large enough to have affected inequality, two caveats are in order. First, immigrants are heavily concentrated in a few states, such as California and Florida. Topel (1994) documents that inequality did rise in these states, but it rose in most areas, even those with very few immigrants. Therefore, other factors must also have been depressing the wages of less-skilled workers. Second, if immigration lowered the wages of less-skilled workers, firms should have hired more of them. As we have seen, this did not happen. Some other factor(s) induced firms to hire fewer low-skilled workers in spite of their lower cost. This is a problem with all supply-side explanations, which accurately predict a decline in the relative wages of the less-skilled, but inaccurately predict an increase in the number of these workers hired.

Behavioral Responses to Government Income Transfers. Another possible supply-side explanation for the increase in inequality, popularized by Murray (1984), is that higher government benefits, especially in income-tested welfare programs, had such large work-disincentive effects that the total earnings of the poor actually fell.

For example, after benefits went up welfare mothers might have worked fewer hours, or their children's fathers, who might have otherwise worked at minimum-wage jobs, might have withdrawn from the labor force.

Moffitt (1990) finds little evidence to support this hypothesis. Because earnings inequality grew in almost all groups, including highly educated men who do not typically receive welfare, this could not be an important explanation. Furthermore, if there were a link between the availability of welfare and inequality of earnings it would come from a change in hours worked. But, as discussed earlier, most of the increased inequality resulted from changes in the distribution of wages, not from changes in the distribution of hours.

Finally, the time series evidence contradicts this hypothesis. The real value of welfare benefits increased rapidly between the early 1960s and the mid-1970s, but fell thereafter (see Figure 2.1 and Danziger and Gottschalk, 1985). If rising welfare benefits distorted work effort and family structure, then falling benefits should have had the opposite effect. Yet there was no reversal in the trend in work effort after real welfare benefits began to fall.[6]

Demand-Side Factors

Declining Skills. One commonly offered explanation of the drop in the wages of recent high school graduates is that the quality of the U.S. educational system has deteriorated. According to this argument, students learn less in school and graduate with fewer marketable skills than their counterparts did in earlier decades. This decline in skills has led employers to hire fewer young high school graduates and to pay them less.

Direct measures of marketable skills are required to test this hypothesis. Such measures are not available, but there is evidence on trends in high school students' test scores. Test scores fell during the 1970s but went up during the 1980s.[7] If these scores measure marketable skills, then according to the hypothesis the wages of high school graduates should have fallen during the 1970s and risen during the 1980s. This is the opposite of what actually happened: real wages of high school graduates fell precipitously during the 1980s.

A more direct refutation of this hypothesis comes from trends in the wages of high school graduates in different cohorts. If wages went down because of poorer schooling in recent years, then the wages of older high school graduates should have been unaffected. In other words, if those who graduated from high school in the 1960s had better skills than those who graduated in the 1980s, then during the 1980s the wages of experienced workers should not have suffered the same decline as those of recent graduates. However, wages went down for high school graduates at all levels of experience.

Business Cycles. If firms want to avoid losing their highly trained workers when business is in a decline, then inequality of earnings will be sensitive to business cycles. During recessions, lower-skilled and lower-paid workers will be more likely to be laid off and will experience larger reductions in hours and wages. During expansions, as these workers are called back to their jobs, their hours and their wages will increase more than those of the stably employed higher-wage workers. The result will be a countercyclical pattern: rising inequality as the economy slows and falling inequality as the economy grows.

Compared with the 1950s and 1960s, the period since 1973 has been characterized by more and larger cyclical swings. How much of the increase in inequality reflects the expected response to business cycles? Until the early 1980s a plausible case could have been made that increased inequality was nothing more than the expected response to the recessions of 1974–1975 and 1980. The 1982–1989 recovery, however, laid this explanation to rest. As the economy emerged from the recession and expanded for seven years, inequality should have declined. This certainly did not happen.

This relationship between the business cycle and earnings inequality is illustrated in Figure 7.2, which plots the unemployment rate for men against their 90/10 ratio.[8] If the increase in inequality were primarily caused by increased unemployment, then when unemployment rates rise, the 90/10 ratio should also rise, and when the economy expands after a recession, both the unemployment rate and inequality should decline. Thus the line in Figure 7.2 should move upward (toward higher inequality) and to

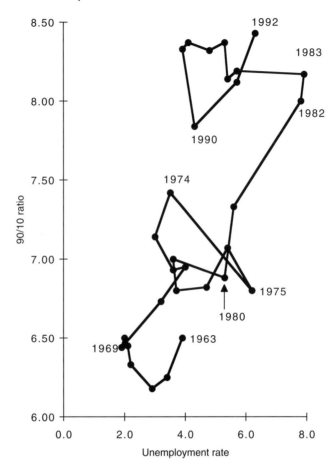

Figure 7.2   Unemployment and 90/10 ratio for men, 1963–1992. (Source: Unemployment data from U.S. Council of Economic Advisers, 1993.)

the right (higher unemployment) during recessions and downward (lower inequality) and to the left (lower unemployment) during expansions.

This pattern did hold through the early 1970s: both unemployment and inequality fell between 1963 and 1965, and the 1969–1970 recession was accompanied by a large increase in inequality. Since then, however, the pattern has changed dramatically. Inequality has gone up during every recession, but it has not fallen during every recovery. The largest increase occurred during the 1981–1982 recession, as the 90/10 ratio climbed from below 7.0 in 1980 to above 8.0 in 1983. After that, inequality continued to rise even as male unemployment rates fell from more than 7 percent in 1983 to about 4 percent in 1989. This pattern indicates that forces other than the business cycle prevented inequality from falling during the expansion of the 1980s.

Economic Restructuring. The past two decades have been marked by substantial changes in the industrial structure of developed economies. The shift of employment out of manufacturing and into the service sector generated two related hypotheses concerning the causes of the increases in inequality. One focused on "deindustrialization" in general; the other on the effects of changes in the global economy, especially increased international competition and the increased openness of the American economy.

According to the deindustrialization hypothesis, changes in industrial structure directly caused distributional changes. In other words, there were fewer jobs for auto workers and more jobs for "hamburger flippers." The resulting shift of workers into industries characterized by both lower average wages and greater disparities in wages would increase overall inequality even if the wages paid within each industry remained unchanged.

This hypothesis is consistent with the data. The decline in the percentage of the workforce in manufacturing mirrors the rise in inequality of men's earnings. Inequality increased as manufacturing declined from about 30 percent to about 20 percent of the workforce between the mid-1960s and the late 1980s. Stories about displaced industrial workers who had to accept lower wages and fewer benefits in the service sector became a staple of the popular press. The correlation between rising inequality and a shift of jobs out of manufacturing is called into question, however, by the fact that inequality increased within most industries. If most of the rise in inequality was attributable to wage changes *within* industries, then shifts in employment *between* industries could explain only a small portion of the total change in inequality.

The evidence that inequality was increasing in all industrial sectors is very strong. Murphy and Welch (1993) document a remarkable increase in demand for college-educated workers in all industries. Between 1970 and 1984 the proportion of the labor force with a college education grew by 13.9 percent, and almost all of the increase (11.6 percent) was accounted for by higher levels of education within industries, rather than by shifts toward industries requiring a higher-educated workforce.[9] The educational upgrading was widespread across industries, including manufacturing, not limited to high-tech or other service-sector industries. Employers were hiring fewer less-skilled workers independent of deindustrialization.

Berman, Bound, and Griliches (1994) also conclude that change in the industrial structure was not the major cause of the increase in inequality. They analyze detailed manufacturing industries and find that industrial restructuring played only a small role in decreasing the demand for less-skilled workers. Employment of production workers in manufacturing dropped 15 percent during the 1980s. But less than one-third of this decline can be explained by the shift away from manufacturing industries that are heavy users of production workers. Most of the change came from shifts away from production workers toward other types of workers *within* narrowly defined manufacturing industries.

According to the second hypothesis, which focuses on the effects of globalization, the increased consumption of imports in the United States, together with the growing tendency of firms to shift part of their production out of the country to take advantage of lower wages, reduced the demand for American-made goods. As a result, less-skilled U.S. workers had to accept lower wages or increase their productivity to compete with less-expensive foreign workers. While globalization raised the demand for high-paid professional workers, such as investment bankers, less-skilled workers experienced reductions in wages and job losses.

The globalization and deindustrialization hypotheses are closely related. Increased international competition may be partially responsible for the industrial restructuring, which in turn may have caused inequality to increase. Foreign competition is thought to have its biggest impact on the wages and employment of low-skilled workers—when international trade increases, firms producing goods that can be made by unskilled workers face the largest increase in competition from abroad. This puts downward pressure on the wages of low-skilled workers and causes employers to seek out labor-saving technologies. At the same time, firms producing skill-intensive goods are able to increase exports, raising the demand for skilled workers.

Increased openness to foreign competition is also blamed for the decrease in manufacturing jobs that offer the opportunity for blue-collar workers to earn their way into the middle class. Many such jobs disappeared altogether as firms "outsourced" the production of components to foreign subsidiaries. Good jobs for less-educated workers disappeared, while high-skilled jobs for workers proficient in the use of computers and robotics and low-skilled jobs in the service industries proliferated. The lucky blue-collar workers who retrained moved into the better jobs. A large part of the workforce, however, had to accept jobs with fewer responsibilities and much lower wages and benefits.

The globalization hypothesis is also consistent with the trend in inequality. Globalization of the economy is measured by imports plus exports, as a percentage of GNP.[10] Inequality increased as the share of the GNP accounted for by traded goods and services increased steadily from about 12 to about 28 percent between the early 1970s and the early 1990s.

The idea that our domestic economic problems were caused by foreign competition was popularized by numerous stories in the popular press about Japanese companies invading U.S. markets. The coincidence of the worsening U.S. trade balance with Japan and increasing awareness of the plight of blue-collar workers, especially automobile and steel workers, led many to conclude that international competition was the primary cause of our economic hardships.

Berman, Bound, and Griliches (1994), however, conclude that changes in employment associated with international trade explain only a small portion—9 percent—of the decreased demand for production workers within manufacturing industries.[11] The vast majority of the shift away from production workers is associated with changes *within* industries that produce domestic consumption goods. Many firms in a variety of industries adopted new production methods that allowed them to manufacture goods using fewer production workers.

Outsourcing of parts for domestically produced goods also has only a modest impact on U.S. wages and employment. Berman, Bound, and Griliches (1994) find outsourcing to be an important reason for lost jobs in the automotive and semiconductor industries, both of which are heavily reliant on subcomponents manufactured in other countries. But when total loss of jobs for production workers in manufacturing is considered, outsourcing is a minor factor. Its effect on employment of production workers with low levels of education in all industries must be even smaller.

Even if industrial restructuring and international trade were important, they could not have been the only factors at work. The declining demand for less-skilled workers would have put downward pressure on their wages, causing the wage differential between less- and more-skilled workers to rise. This demand-side change, however, cannot explain the educational upgrading in almost all industries. As a result of economic restructuring, less-skilled workers laid off in certain industries sought employment in other industries. Firms in industries not directly affected by international trade or restructuring had to pay higher wages for more-educated workers. The rising wages for the skilled and the increased availability of less-educated workers should have induced these firms to substitute, where possible, less-educated workers for college graduates. But, as we showed earlier, firms did just the opposite. In almost all industries, demand for the higher-priced educated workers *increased*. Forces other than deindustrialization must have caused firms to demand more-educated workers in spite of their higher costs.

Technological Changes.   Firms will hire skilled workers, even if their wages increase, if new technologies make these workers sufficiently more productive. For example, the widespread introduction of computers during the 1970s and the explosion of computer applications during the 1980s increased demand for workers who were computer-literate. Firms substituted computers and more-skilled workers for lower-skilled workers whose tasks could now be performed more efficiently with computers. Insurance companies could lay off file clerks; store clerks were no longer required to stamp the price on each box of cereal; checkout clerks no longer had to enter prices in the cash register. Inventory control was simplified, and reordering could be done automatically. In these and other ways, technology (or automation) decreased the value of the skills of workers with lower levels of education and increased demand for workers with more education.

Deindustrialization and technological changes that favor more-skilled workers have similar empirical implications for wage rates. In both cases the skill premium increases as the demand for more-skilled workers increases. These two competing explanations for the increased inequality, however, have different implications for the mix of less-skilled and more-skilled employees within industries. As we argued earlier, the deindustrialization hypothesis implies that employers will demand fewer skilled workers as the cost of skilled workers increases. Technological change has the opposite effect, increasing the demand for skilled workers in spite of their higher cost.

Technological change which raises the productivity of older and more-educated workers faster than that of younger and less-educated workers is consistent with increases in *both* relative wages *and* relative employment of more-skilled labor. If workers with more education are more productive, then firms will hire more of them in spite of their higher costs. This is exactly what happened. Bound and Johnson (1992) examine the causes of the changes in earnings between education groups and between men and women and conclude that changing technology was the principal cause of rising inequality.

There are two objections to the hypothesis that technological change is responsible for the increases in earnings inequality. One is that technological change has not been directly observed or measured; rather, its impact on inequality has been inferred from observations on the increased employment and wages of highly paid workers. As Davis and Topel put it, this hypothesis "is a bit like inferring the existence of Pluto, because Neptune's orbit does not otherwise fit the predictions of theory. Surely, the hypothesis of

Pluto's existence became more compelling when Pluto was actually sighted in a telescope. Likewise, explanations for a rising skill premium that stress skill-biased technical change will become more compelling when we observe Pluto's counterparts on our computer screens" (1993, p. 218).

The general thrust of this objection is correct. The strongest argument for the importance of technological change that has favored college graduates is that it is one of the few explanations of increases in inequality that is consistent with both the increased wages of higher-educated workers and their increased employment in all industries. There is, however, some direct evidence that production methods have changed in a manner that favors more-skilled workers.

Krueger (1993) found that employees who used computers had substantially higher wages than workers with the same characteristics (for example, race, gender, and age) in the same industries who did not use computers. Because more-educated workers are more likely to use computers and because computers became widespread in the 1980s, this evidence supports the proposition that the increased inequality between education and gender groups was affected by an observed change in production technology.

The importance of technological change has also been documented in industry-specific studies. Bailey (1988) found that the textile industry changed from using some of the oldest equipment in 1960 to being second among manufacturing industries in 1980 in terms of newness. The new technologies for turning fiber into fabric required new skills, so employers demanded workers with more skills. At the same time, the number of jobs open to less-skilled workers decreased, causing demand to fall for those already at the bottom of the distribution.

Similarly, Berman, Bound, and Griliches (1994) cite many innovations that reduced demand for production workers but increased demand for skilled workers. For example, numerically controlled machines and industrial robots reduced the employment of blue-collar workers in the aerospace industry. Printing was revolutionized by the introduction of electronic composition: type no longer had to be manually set; instead, information was entered electronically and transmitted to automated presses. Innovations increased the gap not only between blue-collar and white-collar workers but also among white-collar workers. Computer-aided design and computer-aided engineering decreased demand for draftsmen and other less highly paid white-collar occupations.[12]

The other objection to the hypothesis that technological change is responsible for the increase in earnings inequality focuses on timing. Earnings inequality grew most during the 1980s, yet there is little direct evidence that this was a period of particularly rapid technological change. If anything, overall productivity grew at a low rate during the 1970s and 1980s. Low productivity growth does not, however, necessarily imply anything about the extent of technological change. If the new technologies only marginally increased overall productivity, but substantially increased the relative demands for one type of worker over another, they still could have increased inequality.[13]

The issue of the timing of technological change is addressed by Katz and Murphy (1992), who show that the decline in the education premium in the 1970s and its rise in the 1980s is consistent with a rapid but steady secular growth in demand for more-skilled workers over the two decades and a slowing of growth in supply during the 1980s. Because increases in demand outpaced increases in supply during the 1980s, wages rose for more-skilled workers. As is often the case, both supply and demand were important in explaining changes in relative wages.

While technological change may contribute to increases in inequality, it also reduces the cost of many products to consumers. As mentioned earlier, market forces that lead to greater efficiency may have adverse effects on equity. It is left to the public sector to compensate for these undesirable side effects of progress. But the public sector did little to offset the rising inequality generated by the market during the 1980s. In the next chapter we will discuss policies designed to offset the negative side effects of rising wages.

Instability of Earnings.   Thus far our discussion of explanations for the increased inequality of earnings has focused on factors that affect permanent or lifetime wages. For example, if the adoption of new technologies increased the demand for skilled workers, this would permanently raise their relative wages. In any year, however, an individual may experience a temporary increase or decrease in earnings. On the positive side, for example, a worker may receive large bonuses, make more sales, or work more overtime. These factors will create transitory departures from permanent (long-term-average) earnings.

The distinction between permanent and transitory earnings is important. For example, technological change that lowers the demand for less-skilled workers is likely to affect permanent earnings. But increased variation of transitory earnings will also increase inequality of earnings in any year. Suppose the number of workers with low wages increases. This may indicate either that their permanent earnings have dropped or that their earnings have become more volatile, leading some to have temporarily low earnings. If a firm shifts its payment practice toward greater reliance on commissions, average earnings may not change, but earnings variation may increase. The proportion of workers who have low (or high) earnings in any one year will then increase.

Gottschalk and Moffitt (1994) explore whether the increased inequality of yearly earnings partially reflects increases in the variation of transitory earnings. Calculating both average earnings for each individual and deviations from those average earnings in the 1970s and in the 1980s, they find that the variance of permanent and the variance of transitory earnings each increased by about 40 percent. They conclude that one-third to one-half of the increased inequality of yearly earnings in the 1980s can be attributed to increases in earnings variability. Furthermore, this increase in earnings instability was widespread. The variance of transitory earnings increased for all education and age groups, though somewhat more for persons with less education (fewer than twelve years of schooling) and lower permanent earnings (the lowest 25 percent of workers).

We explore three factors that may have contributed to greater instability of earnings: (1) changes in the extent of part-time work, (2) changes in job turnover, especially involuntary turnover, and (3) changes in the use of temporary or contingent workers.

An increase in the percentage of the workforce employed part time is often cited as a sign of deterioration in labor markets during the 1980s. Part-time workers have lower earnings than full-time workers, so an increase in part-time work will increase inequality of annual earnings. Furthermore, if the earnings of part-time workers are more variable than those of full-time workers, then a shift to more part-time workers will increase transitory fluctuations in earnings.[14]

The widespread perception that part-time work became more prevalent during the 1980s, however, is not correct. Among employed men aged 25–54 the proportion who worked part time increased between the late 1970s and early 1980s because of the recession. In the 1980s, however, the period during which earnings became more volatile, the proportion of men working part time remained remarkably constant, at around 5 percent. In contrast, the proportion of employed women who worked part time decreased from around 25 to 21 percent between the early 1980s and the early 1990s.

Part-time workers include both workers who choose to work part time and those who wish to work full time but cannot find satisfactory full-time employment. For both men and women the proportion who worked part time for economic reasons rather than by choice increased sharply in the recession of the early 1980s, then declined during the rest of the decade.

The continued increase in earnings variability during the recovery of the 1980s was, therefore, not primarily caused by changes in the proportion of workers employed part time. At best, the failure of part-time work to return to the level of the 1970s may explain why earnings did not become *less* variable.

Another common perception is that job turnover, especially involuntary turnover associated with plant shutdowns, increased during the 1980s. Because job changes are often accompanied by changes in earnings, an increase in job losses could account for the rise in earnings variability.

Job loss was higher on average in the 1980s than in the 1970s. For the years 1967–1992, Figure 7.3 shows the proportion of the labor force who lost their jobs involuntarily. This includes terminations for business-related reasons such as slack work and plant

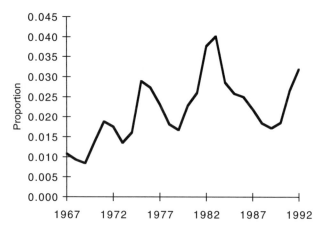

Figure 7.3   Job losers as a proportion of the labor force, 1967–1992. (Source: Medoff, 1993.)

shutdowns, as well as involuntary terminations for cause. The trend is very sensitive to business cycles, and shows sharp spikes during the recessions of the mid-1970s, early 1980s, and early 1990s. The extent of job loss was, however, about the same in 1979 and 1989, the last two cyclical peaks, suggesting that this factor could not have accounted for much of the increase in the variability of earnings.

Job losses always increase during recessions. Levy (1995) and Farber (1993), however, document that highly educated and older workers were more likely to lose their jobs in the 1990–1991 recession than in earlier ones. That is, while job losses were concentrated among the less-skilled, the burden was more widely shared.

This shift reflects changes in the industrial structure of the labor force. Table 7.1 shows the distribution of job losers by industry. While more than 36 percent of those who lost their jobs during 1982–1983 were in manufacturing, only 25 percent were by 1986–1987, and the manufacturing share stayed at this level even during the 1990–1991 recession.[15] Wholesale and retail trade absorbed a large part of the resulting increase in the share of job losers, but the higher-wage financial services and professional services sectors were also affected. This wider distribution of job losses across industrial sectors is consistent with a widely distributed increase in the variability of earnings, especially among more educated workers.

Table 7.1   Share of involuntary job loss by industry

Year	Manufacturing	Trade	Financial services	Professional services	Other
1982–1983	0.37	0.17	0.02	0.06	0.38
1984–1985	0.36	0.16	0.03	0.06	0.39
1986–1987	0.25	0.24	0.05	0.09	0.37
1988–1989	0.25	0.23	0.06	0.10	0.36
1990–1991	0.25	0.21	0.06	0.11	0.37

Source: Farber (1993), p. 88.

Another development in labor markets during the 1980s that may have affected earnings variability is the increased number of workers employed by temporary agencies. Because these workers are less likely than others to work a steady number of hours throughout the year, they experience above-average variation in earnings. If this sector is characterized by higher earnings variability and has grown rapidly, it may have contributed to the rise in earnings variability.[16]

Figure 7.4 compares trends in employment in the temporary help industry with those in the steel and automobile industries. The number of employees in agencies that placed workers in temporary jobs with other firms increased sevenfold between 1972 and 1991, from roughly 200,000 to over 1,400,000. The "temp" industry was as large as the steel industry by 1982.[17] By 1986 it had grown to the size of the auto industry, and in 1992 it was roughly as large as these two industries combined.[18]

Note that the growth of the temporary help industry is secular rather than cyclical. In contrast to the time series on part-time workers and on job losses, which showed strong cyclical components, this series shows a steady upward trend.

Although this industry has historically been composed of office workers, there has been a recent shift to other types of workers and toward higher-paid occupations. Office workers made up two-thirds of all temporary help in 1972 but, a decade later, only slightly more than half. Industrial workers made up roughly one-quarter of all temporary help, and the remaining quarter were technical, professional, and medical workers (Abraham, 1990).

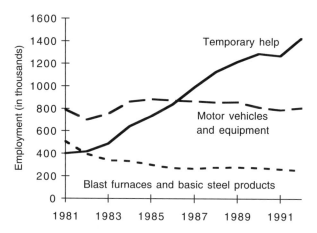

Figure 7.4   Employment in three industries, 1981–1993. (Source: U.S. Bureau of Labor Statistics.)

Temporary help is often—but not always—associated with poorly paid "contingent" work. Clerks and lower-paid occupations do receive lower average wages in this industry than in other industries, but higher-skilled temporary workers actually receive a wage premium (see Abraham, 1990, and Blank, 1990). They may, in fact, be receiving this premium in compensation for the variability in their earnings.

While there is no direct evidence, it seems likely that workers in the temporary services industry experience higher-than-average fluctuations in earnings. Furthermore, the fact that these workers are being placed in a wide variety of jobs suggests that the growth in this industry may be affecting a broad segment of the labor market. Since the temporary help industry accounts for less than 2 percent of the workforce, it is too small to explain much of the increase in earnings variability. It may, however, be an important contributing factor.

Conclusions and Open Questions

Inequality of earnings increased in the 1980s, as employers hired workers with more education in spite of their higher costs and hired fewer less-educated workers even though the wages they would have had to pay them declined. The literature identifies no single cause for the increased earnings inequality of the past two decades. Many factors moved the economy in the same direction: a shrinking percentage of the workforce belonging to unions; a shift of jobs away from manufacturing; increased global competition and the consequent expansion of the import and export sectors. The introduction and widespread use of computers and other technological innovations also increased demand for skilled personnel who could run the more sophisticated equipment. Simultaneously, demand for less-skilled workers declined, as they were displaced by automation or had to compete with new imports.

About half of the increase in earnings inequality for men during the 1980s reflects changes in the distribution of permanent earnings. The other half reflects changes in year-to-year fluctuations. Research in the latter area is in its infancy, as instability of earnings has only recently been recognized as an important contributor to the increases in inequality. Part-time employment is not likely to be an important explanatory factor, as it showed no secular increase during the 1980s. Involuntary terminations may have played a role. Although there was no secular increase in job losses, their burden was spread to a wider segment of the population, making variability in earnings more widely distributed. The growth of the temporary help industry may account for part of the increase in earnings instability, but at this time there is no direct evidence that it does so.

Although there are still gaps in our knowledge, we know more about the dimensions and causes of changes in labor markets than we did in the late 1980s. We know that economic forces outside the control of either firms or politicians contributed to the growth of inequality.

Those economic forces, such as technological change and increased globalization of markets, improve efficiency even as they impose the equity costs we have documented. They have the potential to raise standards of living by introducing new goods and services and reducing prices. Increased returns to skill, which widen the earnings gap between those who have marketable skills and those who do not, also provide incentives for workers to upgrade their skills. Thus these economic changes are not unambiguously bad.

One of government's primary roles is to undertake policies that will offset the inequities arising from these economic changes without introducing unnecessary inefficiencies. In the following chapter we present our recommendations for policies to aid the low-income families who have borne the brunt of the labor market changes of the past two decades.

Chapter 8

An Antipoverty Agenda

The lessons of our economic and policy histories are clear. During the 1950s and 1960s, economic growth raised incomes and reduced poverty. Earnings and family income grew rapidly, and the gains were shared by the poor, the middle class, and the rich. Indeed, the planners of the War on Poverty expected this pattern to continue. They believed that the combination of rapid economic growth and antipoverty policies would raise the incomes of those families who were still outside the economic mainstream.

What they did not foresee was the very different economic situation in which the country found itself beginning in the 1970s. If the rapid and equally distributed economic growth of the postwar period had continued, the vision of the War on Poverty might well have been fulfilled. Even today, if the rate and distributional patterns of economic growth of the 1950s and 1960s could be restored, it would be relatively easy to reduce poverty. Antipoverty programs could then focus primarily on helping those outside the mainstream of economic life, such as the disabled, the aged, residents of depressed areas and regions, and so on. Given a sustained period of sufficiently rapid and even economic growth, plus well-designed antipoverty programs, we could fulfill the predictions of Robert Lampman (1971) and James Tobin (1967) that poverty, as officially measured, could be eliminated.

On the basis of the experiences of the past two decades, however, we doubt that the American economy will return to the patterns of the "good old days" in the foreseeable future. The problem is that since 1973 economic growth has been much slower and much less effective in reducing poverty than it was during the 1950s and 1960s. The gaps between the wages of low-skilled and high-skilled workers have become so large that inequality of earnings and of family income will remain high for many years even if economic conditions improve. As a result, we are not likely to grow our way out of the problems caused by increasing inequality in the labor market. We still need macroeconomic policies that promote economic growth, but we also need enhanced labor market and antipoverty policies to augment the incomes of workers and families who have not benefited from economic growth.

Several lessons from the research and policy experiences of the past thirty years are worth emphasizing. First, there are no simple solutions to the complex problems of poverty and the growing gap between the "haves" and the "have-nots."

One "simple" solution—the negative income tax (NIT), also known as a guaranteed annual income—did receive serious consideration. It was first proposed by Milton Friedman, endorsed by most economists, and later proposed in various forms by Presidents Nixon and Carter. Economists favored the NIT over other antipoverty policies because it would allow recipients greater freedom of choice than would in-kind transfers or social services. It also would not interfere directly in labor markets and would have relatively modest administrative costs. However, strong public feeling against providing cash assistance to those capable of working led to the rejection of this proposal.

Recent polls concerning welfare reform demonstrate that the public favors requiring welfare recipients to work instead of giving them cash assistance, even if such a policy raises total government spending. The public seems willing to pay the child care costs and extra administrative expenses associated with moving recipients into the labor force. That a welfare mother might be more efficient at caring for her own children than at working in the labor market matters little to those whose primary concern is reducing dependence on cash assistance. The failures of the Nixon and Carter administrations to legislate a negative income tax, and the passage of the Family Support Act of 1988, suggest that policies must be consistent with the public's expectations concerning the responsibility of the poor to help themselves as well as with the public's expectations concerning society's responsibility to help the poor.[1]

A second lesson of the past few decades is that education and training programs, which are much more popular with the public than cash assistance, are very expensive. The 1960s was a period of optimism with regard to the effectiveness of such programs in reducing poverty. With little empirical evidence on which to evaluate the claims, it was assumed that these programs would raise the employment and earnings of the disadvantaged. Sayings such as "A fish feeds a family for one meal, but a fishing rod feeds it for a lifetime" expressed the belief that modest government investments in education and training could produce large increases in employment and earnings.

This optimism waned, however, as early evaluations of training programs showed few discernible benefits for participants. Pessimism replaced optimism, and many concluded that such programs did not work. More recent and more careful studies (for reviews see Committee on Youth Employment Programs, 1985; Barnow, 1987; Gueron and Pauly, 1991) have reignited interest in the potential of education and training programs to reduce poverty by increasing the earnings of the least-skilled. Some of these programs have had positive labor market effects large enough to offset their costs.

Government policies to raise wages by improving skills through what are called human capital strategies are very expensive. In a striking calculation, Heckman, Roselius, and Smith (1993) estimate that it would take human capital investments of about $1.7 trillion (in 1989 dollars) to reduce inequalities enough to restore the wage distribution of 1979. Even this calculation is based on the optimistic assumption that these investments would yield a 10 percent annual return via the increased earnings of those receiving education and training.[2]

Even if education and training have only a small impact on the earnings of disadvantaged program participants, increased educational attainment, especially the achievement of a college degree, does have a substantial impact on the earnings of a typical worker.

This was certainly the case in the 1980s, when skilled workers were in relatively short supply at the same time that the demand for their skills had increased.

A third lesson of the last three decades is that market forces alone are not likely to alleviate the economic hardships generated by the labor market—that government action is needed as well. Market forces will lead to some adjustments that, in the long run, may reduce labor market inequalities. For example, the rising returns to education may induce individuals to increase their education and improve their skills. While such a market adjustment is likely to occur in the long run, the wages of the less-skilled are likely to remain low in the interim. In addition, the workers most likely to take advantage of such market trends are those who are young and can afford higher education, not the less-skilled, prime-age workers who also have been hurt by changes in the labor market.

Because such supply-side responses are likely to take so long, and because so many workers have fared badly in the labor market over the past two decades, there is an urgent need for policies that can offset the economic hardships generated by the market without unduly interfering with the market itself. The formulation of these policies will involve all the standard tradeoffs emphasized in economics textbooks. Efficiency costs associated with market interventions and redistributive programs must be balanced against equity gains. Programs that take account of individual needs must be balanced against the need for administrative simplicity. Costs of antipoverty programs must be balanced against other pressing national priorities.

Our primary concern is to improve employment prospects and earnings for those with low skills who want to work. Through no fault of their own, workers in the mid-1990s face much bleaker labor market prospects than did their counterparts in the early 1970s. As we showed in Chapter 6, workers at the bottom of the wage distribution in the early 1990s earned substantially less in real terms than comparable workers two decades earlier. Many workers also face a higher risk of losing their jobs. Those who had the misfortune of being born in the wrong decade found jobs harder to get, and the jobs that were available often paid lower wages, offered less than full-time work, and did not provide pensions or health insurance.

The measures we propose to reduce poverty and labor market inequalities are shaped by these lessons and by the severe constraints imposed on any new federal initiatives by the budget deficit. Both political and fiscal realities limit the scope of what now can be done. Nonetheless, we believe that modest steps should be taken to address the very real needs of those whose employment and earnings have been adversely affected by the changes in the labor market reviewed in Chapters 6 and 7. The history of redistributive income-maintenance strategies has taught us to be wary of attempts to provide cash assistance to the able-bodied without requiring work in return. The history of human capital programs has taught us to be patient, and to be modest in our expectations of what such programs can do for the disadvantaged and/or to be willing to spend very large sums.

We propose an expanded antipoverty initiative that emphasizes assistance to workers. For those who have jobs, we propose expanded wage supplements and child care credits. For those who want to work but cannot find regular employment, we advocate transitional public service jobs paying the minimum wage. These proposals follow from our belief that the American public is willing to spend additional government funds to provide opportunities for the able-bodied poor to work their way out of poverty.

We recognize that some people on welfare or among the unemployed do not take advantage of the labor market opportunities already available to them (Mead, 1992). But we dispute the often-heard assertion that the problems facing low-wage workers in the 1990s are largely of their own making. The evidence reviewed in earlier chapters demonstrates that structural changes in the economy have caused employers' demand for labor to shift away from less-skilled workers. Jobs are now harder to find, and many of the ones that can be found pay lower real wages and provide fewer benefits than similar jobs in the early 1970s. As a result, some workers have given up and withdrawn from the labor force.[3] The policies we propose are directed toward the workers who have been most affected by these changes. They would supplement the earnings of low-wage workers, increase the employment prospects of the jobless, and offset some of the detrimental impacts of the slow growth and rising inequality of the past two decades.

Our proposals differ in two important respects from those aimed at increasing work incentives and work requirements for welfare recipients. First, our proposals are addressed not just to people on welfare but to *all workers* adversely affected by economic changes. Only a small portion of those whose labor market prospects have diminished since the early 1970s receive welfare benefits. The measures we propose also include those who have suffered economic losses associated with labor market changes and who either have been ineligible for welfare or have chosen not to participate.

Second, our proposals focus on earnings supplements and work opportunities rather than work incentives or work requirements. That is, they emphasize changes in the demand side of the labor market. In our view, the problem is not that more people have chosen not to work, but rather that demand by employers for less-skilled workers, even those who are willing to work at low wages, has declined. We find it paradoxical that so much attention has been focused on changing the labor-supply behavior of welfare recipients and so little has been given to changing the demand side of a labor market that has been increasingly unable to employ less-skilled and less-experienced workers.

Our policies would ensure that a family with at least one full-time worker earning the minimum wage would have an income above the poverty line, after taxes and child care expenses. There are two components to this antipoverty strategy—policies to supplement the earnings of low-wage workers and policies to alleviate the employment problems of low-wage workers who cannot find full-time work. For the latter group, the labor market problems are more acute and the proposed policy solutions are both more controversial and more expensive.[4]

In 1991, according to our poverty measure, there were 31.1 million poor persons in the U.S. population (see Figure 8.1). Of those, 9.5 million lived in families in which the heads were over 65 years of age, disabled, ill, or in school (and therefore might not be expected to work); our proposals focus on the remaining 21.6 million, those living in families whose heads might be expected to work.[5]

Of those 21.6 million poor persons, 19 percent live in families whose heads work full time, full year. (For purposes of discussion,

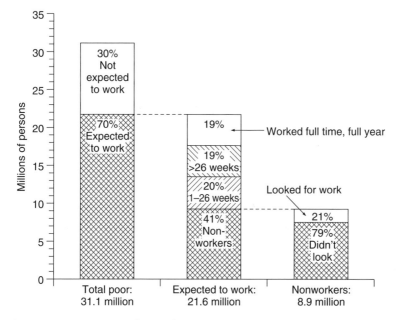

Figure 8.1 Poor persons by work status of head of family, 1991. (Source: Authors' calculations from March 1992 Current Population Survey.)

we will treat the 1991 figures as current and refer to them in the present tense.) Their problem is low wages, not lack of work.[6] The best way to reduce poverty for these families is to reform the federal personal income tax to supplement their earnings. Another 39 percent live in families whose heads work less than full time, full year. These families can potentially benefit both from policies designed to supplement earnings and from those designed to expand employment opportunities.

Another 8.9 million poor persons live in families whose heads have no labor market income. About one-fifth of the 8.9 million live with family heads who indicate a desire to work: that is, they reported either that they looked for work during the year or that they did not look because they did not believe they could find a job. These families could also benefit from the employment policies we propose.

These figures provide only a rough measure of the proportion of the poor who could be aided by the policies we propose. Because our focus is on *all* those who have been adversely affected by recent labor market changes, we have not considered sex or marital status or childrearing responsibilities in distinguishing between those who might want to work and those who might not. For example, if we had categorized single mothers with young children as not expected to work (see Danziger and Gottschalk, 1986), their families would not be counted among those who would benefit from our proposed policies. Also, although in these rough figures all family heads who did not look for work are counted together, as if they do not want to work, in fact other factors, such as lack of marketable skills or problems with child care or transportation, may have kept many of them from looking for jobs. If our proposed policies reduced such barriers, the latter group and their families would be added to the category of those the policies might benefit.[7]

According to our admittedly rough calculation, then, of the 31.1 million poor persons in 1991, 41 percent lived with family heads who worked at some point during the year and 6 percent with heads who looked for work but did not find it. Our policies are targeted on these 47 percent: the roughly 14.5 million poor persons in families with heads who are working or looking for work.

Rewarding Work

The Earned Income Tax Credit

As discussed in Chapter 6, the real wages of low-skilled workers fell substantially between the early 1970s and the early 1990s. During this period, a policy was enacted (and became quite popular) that provides a way to offset wage declines for low-income workers. The Earned Income Tax Credit (EITC) was enacted in 1975, and expanded in 1986, 1990 and 1993. It has retained bipartisan support because of a number of its features: it assists only those who work; it helps two-parent as well as single-parent families; it raises the employee's take-home pay without increasing the employer's labor costs. In 1993 a low-income worker who resided with two or more children was eligible for a refundable tax credit of up to 19.5 cents for each dollar of earnings. (A refundable tax credit is one that provides payments, or "refunds," even to those families who owe no taxes.) This meant that a job paying the minimum wage of $4.25 was worth up to $5.08, taking into account the value of the EITC.[8]

An expanded EITC is a key to "making work pay." In 1993 President Clinton proposed and Congress enacted a major expansion. The new provisions, to be phased in between 1994 and 1996, will provide an additional $21 billion to the working poor and near-poor over five years. This legislation raised the credit rate, the maximum credit, and the income level over which benefits are available. By 1996, for every dollar earned, the EITC will provide an additional 40 cents (for families with two or more children) up to a maximum of $3,560 for workers earning between $8,900 and $11,620 (see Figure 8.2).[9] This will make the minimum wage, supplemented by the EITC, equal to $5.95 for these families. The credit will then be reduced at a rate of 21 cents per dollar for earnings above $11,620, so that it will phase out at $28,524. As Figure 8.2 indicates, a similar pattern will apply for families with one child.

The 1993 Act also provided, for the first time, a small EITC for childless workers between the ages of 24 and 65 (shown at the bottom of Figure 8.2). Their EITC, beginning in 1994, is 7.65 cents for every dollar earned up to $4,000. The maximum benefit, $306, just offsets the employee's share of the Social Security payroll tax, which is 7.65 percent, over this income range. From $5,000 to $9,000, the EITC for single workers is phased out, and the EITC is less than their Social Security taxes.

This expansion of EITC is substantial. In 1993, before the expansion, 14 million families claimed credits of about $13 billion. By 1996, an additional 4.7 million families will be eligible and the total credit will amount to about $25 billion. The EITC will then provide about the same amount of cash assistance as the AFDC program (U.S. House of Representatives, Committee on Ways and Means, 1994). The expanded EITC will remove an additional 2.4 million persons from poverty.[10]

When fully implemented, the expanded EITC will substantially offset the decline in real wages over the past two decades for workers at the bottom of the earnings distribution who work year-round and reside in families with children. Single workers and childless couples, however, need greater earnings supplementation than the

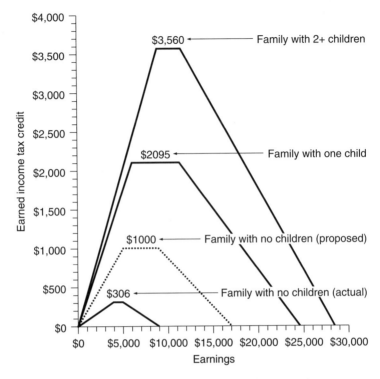

Figure 8.2   Earned income tax credit, 1996. (Source: 1994 *Green Book*, p. 700.)

1993 law provides to offset the increase in their Social Security taxes and the decline in their wages over this period. Therefore, we propose additional wage supplements for the working poor who are still not adequately covered by the 1993 law. We would expand the EITC for single workers and childless couples, as indicated in Figure 8.2. And we would expand government subsidies for the costs of child care; this would aid a group with a very high poverty rate— single-parent families.

Expanded EITC for Single Workers and Childless Families
The extension of a small EITC to childless workers in the 1993 legislation represents a step in the right direction, as childless low-wage

workers have also experienced large real declines in earnings. By 1996, however, these workers will receive only about $300 from the EITC, whereas similar workers with children will receive about $3,000. Although there is a good rationale for more generous treatment of families with children, this disparity is too large.

Families with children have always been treated more generously by tax and transfer policies than childless persons of working age, for several reasons. One is that the public tends to consider poor adults responsible for their own poverty, but to consider poor children "truly needy" and not responsible for their disadvantages. Another reason is the belief that expenditures on children represent an investment in the future productivity of the nation's labor force— that society can raise the educational attainment, employment, and earnings of the next generation of workers through investments in children. The substantial expansion of the EITC over the decade 1986–1996 was motivated by the high poverty rate of children and reflected these broad social objectives.

In contrast, there has been virtually no discussion of the economic needs of low-income single workers and childless families. This probably has more to do with the large budget deficits than with an analysis of the needs of the working poor with children relative to those of the childless working poor.

The next logical step in making the EITC a major component of antipoverty policy is to expand assistance for childless workers. An expansion to include all persons regardless of age or family status would be expensive, however, and might provide tax credits to persons who have low annual earnings but are not poor, such as students or grown children living with their parents. The 1993 law attempts to address this problem by restricting the EITC for childless persons to those between the ages of 25 and 64. An expansion of the EITC for childless workers in this age range would offer an excellent opportunity to assist those who have been left behind by the slow growth and rising inequality of the past two decades.

For childless couples, we would raise the subsidy from 7.65 to 20 cents per dollar of earnings, with a maximum payment of $1,000 for workers earning between $5,000 and $9,000. The credit would be reduced at a 15 percent rate so that it would be phased out at earnings of close to $17,000. For single workers, we would raise the subsidy to 15 cents per dollar, with a maximum of $750 for workers earning between $5,000 and $9,000. Above that level it would be reduced by 15 cents per dollar of earnings, phasing out at $14,000. As Figure 8.2 shows, this would be a substantial expansion for childless workers. Most EITC payments would still benefit families with children. Our proposal would raise the earnings of about 9.5 million single workers and childless couples, and would cost the Treasury about $5 billion per year.[11]

Refundable Income Tax Credits for the Working Poor

On its own, the expanded EITC will not be sufficient to keep many families with children out of poverty. The 1994 poverty line for a family of three was about $12,500 and that for a family of four about $15,500. A family of four with a full-time minimum-wage worker would have had income of $8,500 from earnings and, if the 1996 EITC had been in effect in 1994, would have received credits of $3,370. The family would also have been eligible for about $2,400 in food stamps. It would not have owed any federal income tax, but would have paid $650 in Social Security taxes, resulting in a disposable income of about $13,650 if it did not have child care expenses, less if it did.[12] Thus, a family of three with one full-time earner and modest child care costs would have had income above the poverty line, but a four-person family would not.[13]

Several additional policy changes are needed if we are to guarantee that those who work will not be poor. One possible change would be to raise the minimum wage. If the minimum wage were increased to $5.15 per hour, for example, as President Clinton proposed in 1995, a full-time minimum-wage worker would receive $10,300 in earnings, $3,370 from the EITC, and about $2,200 in food stamps, and would pay $788 in Social Security taxes. This would raise a family of four very close to the poverty line. Increases in the minimum wage, however, are very controversial. Employers object because a higher minimum wage raises their costs. Many economists object because increases in the minimum wage can reduce employment and because most minimum-wage workers do not live in poor families.[14]

We are not opposed to increasing the minimum wage. However, an alternative policy would be more effective in aiding working-poor families with children. Because child care expenses can account for a substantial portion of the income of low-wage families (Hofferth, 1995), federal subsidies for child care should be expanded. This is particularly important for low-wage single parents and for secondary earners in low-income two-parent families. We therefore propose to expand the existing Dependent Care Credit (DCC) and to make it refundable.

The DCC is a nonrefundable income tax credit. A taxpayer may claim the credit for expenses, incurred for a child under age 13, that are required for the taxpayer to work. All working single parents with qualifying dependents are eligible for the DCC. Two-parent families can claim the credit only when both parents work.[15]

The expenses claimed cannot exceed $2,400 if there is one dependent or $4,800 if there are two. Families with incomes below $10,000 can claim a nonrefundable tax credit of 30 percent of child care expenses up to a maximum credit of $720 for one child and $1,440 for two or more children. The credit is then reduced for families with higher incomes until it reaches $480 for one child ($960 for two children) for parents earning $20,000 or more per year. The intent of the credit is to reduce the costs of working for all families with children. However, the working poor gain very little from the nonrefundable DCC because they typically owe no federal income tax. (A nonrefundable tax credit reduces taxes owed, but provides no further benefits to those owing no taxes.) Most of the almost $3 billion of the credit claimed in 1994 accrued to about 6 million middle-income and high-income families whose income tax liabilities enabled them to take full advantage of the credit.

The solid lines in Figure 8.3 show the maximum value of this nonrefundable credit under current law for working single parents who claim the standard deduction. Because a single-parent family does not owe federal income tax until its adjusted gross income exceeds $10,000, the value of the credit is zero below this income.[16] As income rises, the taxpayer begins to pay 15 cents for each additional dollar earned, while the DCC falls from about 30 percent of child care costs at $10,000 to 20 percent for incomes above $20,000.

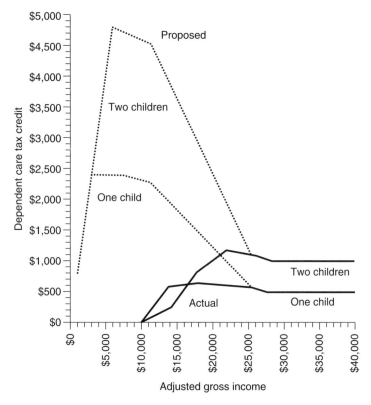

Figure 8.3   Dependent care tax credit claimable for single-parent families with maximum allowable child care expense eligible for credit. (Source: 1993 *Green Book*, pp. 1068–1069.)

As a result the value of the credit increases, then falls slightly, reaching $480 for the family with one child and $960 for the family with two children.

Many of the working poor, especially those with preschoolers, spend a substantial portion of their income on child care. For others, particularly single mothers who can find only low-wage jobs, high child care costs are a major deterrent to work. For example, without some child care subsidy, a single mother with two young children is unlikely to accept a full-time job paying $10,000 per year if she faces daycare costs of $4,000. (In fact for two children $4,000 is a low estimate, only about $1.00 per hour per child.) In some states she will have more disposable income, from welfare, food stamps, and Medicaid, if she does not work than if she does. If the current DCC were refundable, however, she would receive a $1,200 credit for child care expenses. Steffick and Giannarelli (1993) estimate that changing the current DCC from nonrefundable to refundable would have aided an additional 1.1 million low-income families at a cost of about $700 million in 1994.

Even if the DCC were made refundable, however, the 30 percent maximum subsidy rate is too low, given the costs of daycare, to "make work pay" for workers at the bottom of the wage distribution. We would raise the maximum subsidy to 80 percent of child care costs for families earning less than $10,000, and then lower the rate by 4 percent for every $1,000 earned so it would be 40 percent for families earning $20,000 and 20 percent for families earning $25,000 or more.[17] Given the high cost of child care, we would also raise the maximum allowable expenses to $3,000 per year for one child and $6,000 for two or more children. Our proposal is shown by the dotted lines in Figure 8.3.

Under this scenario, the single mother earning $10,000 and spending $4,000 on care for her two children would receive a refundable credit of $3,200. A family with two children earning $25,000 would be eligible for a maximum credit of $1,200, as compared to a maximum of $960 today. Thus most of the added subsidies for child care resulting from this proposal would aid poor and near-poor working families. We estimate that such a DCC expansion would cost the Treasury an additional $5 billion per year.[18] Taken together, the recently expanded EITC and a refundable DCC would go a long way toward reducing poverty in families with children in which the parents work at low wages.[19]

State Income Tax Relief for the Working Poor

State governments could also help working poor families by incorporating refundable credits into their tax systems. The Family Support Act of 1988 requires states to design welfare-to-work programs to encourage recipients to leave welfare. Most of these programs emphasized changes *within* welfare that make continued dependency less desirable. All of the reforms we have mentioned would raise the standard of living of workers relative to that of welfare recipients through changes *outside* welfare. Refundable state tax credits are an additional way to make work more attractive than welfare.

Refundable credits would be particularly appropriate in state tax systems for two reasons. First, states tend to raise a large share of their revenues through sales taxes—a form of tax that falls disproportionately on low-income families. Second, while the federal government has removed the working poor from the income tax rolls, many states continue to tax the working poor. For example, in Michigan in 1991 a family of four began owing state income taxes when its income reached $8,400, well below the poverty line of $13,812. By 1991 only six states had adopted earned income credits to assist the working poor.[20]

Expanding Employment Opportunities

While changes in tax policy over the past decade have made significant progress in offsetting the decline in the real earnings of low-wage workers with children, the picture is much bleaker on the employment side. As we showed earlier, in 1991 about 80 percent of the poor lived in families whose heads were capable of working but either did not work or worked less than the full year. Increases in the EITC will take a family out of poverty only if it has the equivalent of one member working full time, full year at the minimum wage. Finding full-time year-round work has become increasingly difficult for less-skilled workers. Inasmuch as employment is still a significant part of the poverty problem, supplementing low wages can be only one part of the solution.

Employer Subsidies

One strategy for improving the employment prospects of less-skilled persons is to provide direct subsidies to private firms that hire low-wage workers. Lowering the cost to firms of hiring a specific group might be beneficial in two ways. First, firms might find it profitable to hire the subsidized less-skilled workers instead of more-skilled workers wherever possible. Second, reducing total costs might enable the firm to expand output. This could lead to increased employment of all groups, including less-skilled workers. (For more on the potential benefits of subsidies to employers, see Phelps, 1994; Haveman, 1988; and Lerman, 1988.)

This argument is correct if two conditions are satisfied. First, firms must be able to substitute easily among different types of workers. Although immediate replacement of skilled workers by less-skilled workers may be limited, firms may eventually switch to different production methods to take advantage of the subsidies. Second, firms must not interpret the wage subsidy as a sign that the subsidized workers' productivity is low. A firm is not likely to hire a worker who costs 25 percent less than a nonsubsidized worker but is also thought to produce 25 percent less. Whether these two conditions are met is an empirical question.

The existing evidence on subsidies to employers is not promising. The United States has experimented with a variety of tax credits to encourage firms to change their hiring patterns. The Targeted Jobs Tax Credit (TJTC) offers credits to firms that hire workers from specific groups that have experienced disadvantages in the labor market (youth from low-income households, Vietnam veterans, some disabled workers, some welfare recipients). The Youth Incentive Entitlement Pilot Projects provided subsidies to employers in selected inner-city areas who hired local young people; the recently enacted Urban Empowerment Zones program also offers subsidies to employers in specified urban zones who hire local residents (Lehman, 1994). Surprisingly few firms participated in TJTC or the Youth Incentive projects (the Urban Empowerment Zones program is too new to have been evaluated), even though they offered subsidies paying 20 to 100 percent of the wage bill (Hahn and Lerman, 1985).

There is evidence suggesting that at least part of the reason firms were unresponsive to these incentives was that they interpreted the wage subsidy as a sign that the subsidized workers would not be good employees. Two experiments, the Dayton Employment Opportunity Pilot Program (EOPP) and the Work Incentive Program

(WIN), provided randomly selected job applicants with vouchers that employers could redeem for tax credits. In both experiments, applicants eligible for the credit were less likely to receive a job offer than members of the control group (see Burtless, 1986; Bishop, 1989). This suggests that employers either view subsidized workers as less productive or are concerned that acceptance of the subsidies will lead to greater governmental scrutiny of their firms (Hollister and Haveman, 1991).[21]

These studies have diminished the attractiveness of subsidies to employers as a strategy to improve job prospects for low-skill workers. Another concern about such subsidies is that employers will take the subsidy for hiring workers they would have hired anyway (Hollister and Haveman, 1991). Given these concerns, we do not propose an expansion of current subsidy programs. There may be some innovative ways to stimulate private demand for low-skill workers, but these should be tested in demonstration projects before being implemented on a wider scale.

Public Service Employment

If private firms are unwilling or unable to hire all poor adults who are willing to accept minimum-wage jobs, even when the government is willing to subsidize them, then society must either accept the higher poverty rate or provide cash assistance and/or employment to the jobless. In view of the public's preference for work over welfare as an antipoverty strategy, and because we believe the high poverty rate is unacceptable, we propose a substantial program of public service employment (PSE). We recognize that there are efficiency costs of and limitations to PSE and that it should not be held out as a panacea. But we think the best way to increase the demand for low-skilled workers is to offer minimum-wage jobs of last resort to poor adults.

PSE programs came under attack in the early 1980s, as the Reagan administration sought to reduce government intervention in the labor market. One criticism was that earlier PSE efforts had not improved the financial status of participants by very much. The consensus from evaluations was that a year of public service employment raised the future annual earnings of women by between

$600 and $1,000 a year in the early 1980s (Barnow, 1987; Gueron and Pauly, 1991). For men the impact was closer to $300 per year. This was hardly enough to turn disadvantaged workers into middle-class taxpayers, and certainly not enough to make the program pay for itself through increased tax revenues or decreased welfare payments.

Is this a definitive argument against PSE? We think not. Although a focus on the magnitude of future returns is appropriate for evaluating education and training programs, it is not necessarily appropriate for evaluating PSE as a job of last resort for those who will not be hired by private employers. Education and training programs are one way to combat market imperfections that prevent low-wage workers from borrowing against future earnings to pay for their training. For example, youth from low-income families may not be able to afford higher education. On grounds of efficiency, the government should encourage them to increase their education if the returns to education are high enough to cover the costs. A similar case on efficiency grounds can be made for PSE. For example, a year of employment in a PSE program might give workers the experience they need to get private employers to hire them. In this case, future returns are a perfectly legitimate basis for evaluating employment programs as well as training programs. If the returns outweigh the costs, then this governmental intervention leads to a more efficient outcome.

But efficiency is not the only reason for supporting PSE. In fact, most arguments in favor of PSE, including the one we emphasize here, are made on the basis that PSE would promote equity, regardless of its effects on efficiency. Poor persons who seek employment deserve the opportunity to work, even if no private employer is willing to hire them. Employing these workers in PSE jobs is by definition a success in this case, quite apart from any impact it may have on their future employment prospects or earnings. After all, if an unemployed person finds a private-sector job, this is usually considered a successful outcome, even if the job has no effect on the person's future wages. In other words, the objective of PSE as an antipoverty program is to allow poor workers to escape poverty by working at minimum-wage jobs. Its success in meeting this objective should be measured not by future returns but by the number of poor people who take PSE jobs.

From this perspective, PSE can be viewed as a way to give people who want to work the opportunity to work, not as an investment intended to increase future, as well as current, earnings. Just as the EITC raises the incomes of low-wage workers who have jobs, PSE offers work to and thus raises the earnings of those who do not have jobs. Neither policy needs to claim substantial impacts on future labor market outcomes to be considered successful.

PSE developed a bad reputation not only because it was oversold, but also because it had some undesirable consequences that either had not been anticipated or had not been acknowledged. For example, evidence from the 1970s indicates that PSE did little to increase the aggregate number of jobs in the economy because the states, localities, and nonprofit organizations that received federal grants to provide PSE jobs gradually substituted PSE workers for unsubsidized employees on their payrolls (Johnson, 1978). It is estimated that after two years of this "fiscal substitution" the local governments and organizations provided their usual levels of services, but those services were now delivered by federally funded PSE workers. The organizations did not maintain their initial workforces and use the subsidized workers to expand services as the program planners had intended.

Another form of substitution can occur through the product market. If PSE workers provide useful goods, they will compete with private-sector providers of these goods. To avoid displacing other workers, PSE workers must be employed to produce only those goods and services not produced in the private sector.[22] For this reason PSE workers, almost by definition, tend to be kept from providing goods that are valued in the market. The program is then criticized for offering only "make-work" assignments.

These criticisms have led many analysts to conclude that PSE is not an efficient way to aid workers in poor households. We disagree because we believe a PSE program can be designed to limit the undesirable consequences.

For example, fiscal substitution occurs when program operators can shift spending on specific projects from the local to the national level. If programs were financed and administered by the same level of government, this substitution problem would not arise. If a PSE program in which the federal government provided all the job slots turned out to be politically unacceptable, then time limits on grants to local governments could reduce fiscal substitution. For example, if local governments could apply only for short-term, nonrenewable projects, say for grants that lasted for no more than two years, they would be less likely to substitute PSE workers for their existing workforce.

While we believe that the arguments against PSE are often over-stated, we agree that it is an imperfect tool. It is, however, the best tool for dealing with a labor market problem that has considerably worsened over the past two decades—high unemployment rates for low-skill workers who cannot find private employers who will hire them. And, given the public's dislike of cash assistance programs, jobs programs, with all their faults, are a relatively popular anti-poverty strategy (Heclo, 1994; Bobo and Smith, 1994).

Our PSE program would have two components. First, we would expand the summer jobs programs for inner-city youth. By defini-tion, these are short-term programs with limited opportunity to dis-place regular public-sector employees. When such programs have offered minimum-wage jobs, they have been flooded with appli-cants. For example, the Youth Incentive Entitlement Pilot Projects, which ran from 1978 to 1981 in seventeen geographic areas, guar-anteed all low-income youths in the area minimum-wage jobs, part time during the school year and full time during the summer, provided that they stayed in school. About 70,000 youths, nearly two-thirds of those eligible, participated. This counters a common perception that young people in the inner city do not want jobs. Hollister and Haveman (1991) conclude that this suggests that youths are willing to work at the minimum wage, but that em-ployers are unwilling to hire all of those willing to work.

The second component of our PSE program would offer a sub-minimum-wage public service job to any applicant. The wages would be set at 10–15 percent below the minimum wage to en-courage movement into available minimum-wage private-sector jobs. The entry-level wage would be about $3.60–$3.85 per hour, which with the EITC would yield roughly the minimum wage for a childless worker, or about $5.30 per hour for a worker with a dependent child.[23] Graduated job ladders would provide rewards to workers who succeeded on the job, but wages would always be lower than an equally successful worker would receive in the private sector. Employees who failed to meet minimal performance standards would be dismissed, and would not be eligible to reapply for six months.

Because the federal government has not operated any PSE programs since the early 1980s, we would be cautious in implementing our program. For example, we might conduct an experiment in which the number of PSE jobs was limited to 250,000–500,000. PSE jobs, including wages, materials, and administrative expenses, are likely to cost about $12,000 each. An experiment with 250,000 jobs would cost about $3 billion per year. While the cost of this program may seem high, it is important to recognize that the United States spends much less on direct job creation and employment subsidies than other industrialized countries.[24] Such an experiment would recognize the relatively high costs of a PSE program and would yield important information about the magnitude of the demand by the poor for low-wage jobs of last resort and about the job performance and productivity of today's jobless workers. We currently have little evidence to counter claims that many of the unemployed do not want to work or that government cannot operate an effective PSE program.

If the experiment proved successful, we would have a much better basis for expanding the program. As Figure 8.1 suggested earlier, demand for public jobs of last resort could be as high as several million. Such a large program, however, would not be budgetarily and administratively feasible at the present time.

We should reemphasize that the program we envision is *not* designed specifically for welfare recipients. Any poor person who wants work and cannot find a minimum wage private-sector job would be included. The welfare reform plan proposed by the Clinton administration in 1994 but set aside when Republicans gained control of Congress in the 1994 elections is, however, relevant to a discussion of PSE jobs of last resort.[25] The Clinton proposal would have changed welfare from an open-ended entitlement to a transitional system under which cash assistance could be received for no more than two years. For those who reached the time limit but could not find work, transitional public jobs would have been available.

A program offering jobs of last resort *only* to welfare recipients who exhaust two years of cash assistance would have the potential for perverse incentives and serious inequities. Families who either were not eligible for welfare or chose not to participate would not have access to these jobs. Even if the incentive to go on welfare in order to gain access to the PSE jobs were small, offering jobs to welfare recipients but not to equally needy families who were trying to make it in the labor market could cause resentment. Thus the Clinton proposal opens debate on the issue of broader access to jobs of last resort.

We should also emphasize that the PSE jobs we are proposing cannot be the "good jobs" that we might wish every worker to have. They are minimal jobs offered as a safety net to poor persons who want to work but are left out of the private labor market. They would not provide solutions to many other pressing problems that many of these employees might have. However, the low earnings from the PSE job, together with the wage supplements we have described, could raise the standard of living of full-time workers close to the poverty line. That is more than we can say for the current system, which offers a minimum wage if you find a job, but leaves millions of poor persons searching for work and many others poor even though they have jobs.

Why have policies to increase work opportunities for low-wage workers and to subsidize their wages received so little attention? And why were public service jobs eliminated in the early 1980s, just as demand for less-skilled workers was falling? Part of the answer reflects the political perspective of that time. The Reagan and Bush administrations had a strong aversion to government interventions in the labor market in general and to public service employment in particular. Bassi and Ashenfelter (1986) show that federal funding for employment and training programs was cut by more than two-thirds between 1979 and 1984. The Job Training Partnership Act (JTPA) was established to encourage the private sector to hire disadvantaged workers. But JTPA is smaller than the jobs program of the 1970s and provides no wages to trainees or any type of public employment.

While ideology is an important reason for the lack of a federal jobs strategy for the poor, it is not the only reason. Before the late 1970s there was little need for public service jobs during expansionary periods because economic growth was rapid and the gains from growth were widely shared. During this period PSE was thought of as primarily a counter-cyclical policy to be put in place during recessions and retired during recoveries. It is only since the late 1970s that the disadvantaged have been left behind during recoveries. The labor market changes we have described seem to have permanently reduced private-sector demand for less-skilled workers. Until these labor market changes are reversed or until the next generation can upgrade its skills before entering the labor market, many workers will be unable to find jobs unless the government becomes an employer of last resort.

Child Support for Single-Parent Families

Improving employment prospects, supplementing low wages, and subsidizing child care costs will go a long way toward redressing the labor market disadvantages faced by less-skilled workers. These policies, however, will not be sufficient to reduce poverty in many single-parent families. Therefore we propose an additional reform, one that would primarily be financed by the absent parents of poor children—an expanded system of child support.[26]

Over the past thirty years the percentage of children living in single-parent families has risen dramatically. As we showed in Chapter 4, these children experience the highest poverty rates of any demographic group: in 1991, about 40 percent of white children and about 65 percent of black and Hispanic children living in mother-only families were poor.

Currently only 60 percent of noncustodial parents have a legal obligation to pay child support, and only half of those meet this obligation in full. Nearly a quarter fail to pay anything. Thus over half of the 16 million children living in single-parent families receive no financial support from their noncustodial parents (Garfinkel, 1992). One promising attempt to correct this problem is the effort to make absent parents more responsible for the support of their children.

Some steps in this direction have already been taken. Greater enforcement of current child support obligations was a feature of the 1988 Family Support Act. An example of a more comprehensive reform, the Downey/Hyde Child Support Enforcement and Assurance Proposal, was introduced in Congress (but not enacted) in 1992. The legislation was based on the child support assurance system (CSAS) developed by Irwin Garfinkel (Garfinkel and McLanahan, 1986; Garfinkel, 1992). CSAS would require absent parents to contribute a fixed percentage of their income to the custodial parent, with the percentage rising with the number of children. The custodial parent would be assured a minimum level of child support; where the absent parent's expected contribution was low, it would be supplemented by government funds up to the assured level. The combination of this support and earnings would keep many single mothers and their children out of poverty.[27] The Downey/Hyde proposal offered an important extension of CSAS that is consistent with our proposed PSE initiative: it would have provided an absent father who could not find a private-sector job with public employment so that he could earn enough to make child support payments.[28]

If the government could do a better job of enforcing current child support obligations, then the amount of child support paid could be increased by over 40 percent, from $7 billion to $10 billion per year. And if child support obligations could be extended to all absent parents, an additional $20 billion could be raised (Oellerich, Garfinkel, and Robins, 1991). Much of this support would go to children who are not poor. It would do much to raise the living standards of children whose single mothers are working but earning modest incomes. These sums are significant even when compared to the public funds that would be made available through an expanded EITC and a refundable child care credit.

Conclusion

The popular belief that anyone who works hard can get ahead in America fosters the view that those who remain poor must be personally responsible for their poverty. Behavioral trends, such as increases in out-of-wedlock childbearing, divorce, and participation in illegal rather than legal economic activities, do contribute to keeping the poverty rate high. But poverty remains high primarily because of the major economic trends of the past two decades—the slow growth and rising inequality that have made it more and more difficult for many families to escape poverty. Another contributing factor has been the lack of public policies to counter those trends.

Our appraisal of what government policies can accomplish suggests that there are several areas in which we already know what needs to be done. We recognize that government cannot quickly solve all poverty and labor market problems because there are just not enough proven policies, especially in public service employment, that can be taken off the shelf and put into practice. We also recognize that our proposals would be expensive, with the entire package costing about $20 billion per year in additional spending. We hope to see a commitment and funding to move forward in those areas where we know what works and funds for demonstration projects in those areas where we need more information.

The policies we propose would directly address the hardships that slow and uneven growth have imposed on our nation's poorest citizens. Supplementing wages and reducing child care costs for those who work, reforming the child support system, and providing jobs of last resort for those who cannot find even minimum-wage work would establish a much more effective safety net than we now have. If the conditions of the 1950s and 1960s, when the private economy rapidly generated job opportunities and higher real wages across the board, ever return, such a safety net will be less essential. But if the patterns of the past two decades continue through the 1990s, then the policies we have proposed could provide vital aid to tens of millions of Americans. It is imperative that our society address the adverse consequences of slow growth and rising inequality.

A Note on the Data

The U.S. Bureau of the Census has published Current Population Survey (CPS) data on the level and distribution of income for families and unrelated individuals annually since 1947, and on poverty rates annually since 1959. Published volumes are also available that report income distributions from the Decennial Censuses of 1950 and each subsequent Census. Data on median and mean family income and several measures of income inequality and poverty are published each year by the Census Bureau in the Current Population Reports, Consumer Income, Series P-60. These reports provide tabulations of data on roughly 60,000 families and unrelated individuals who are interviewed in March about the sources and amount of income they received during the previous calendar year.

Microeconomic data from the CPS and the Census became available to researchers in the form of public use computer tapes in the 1970s. These data allow us to address a variety of questions that cannot be answered with the published data: to examine trends in the level and distribution of various components of income (for example, husbands' earnings, wives' earnings, government transfer payments), or for distinct demographic groups (such as nonelderly two-parent families, mother-only families, the elderly); and to analyze the effects of economic, demographic, and policy changes on trends in poverty and income inequality.

Defining Income. Family income is defined as the sum of money income from all sources during the previous calendar year for all family members residing in the household in March. Money income includes wages and salaries, self-employment income, property income (such as interest, dividends, net rental income), cash benefits received from government income maintenance programs (such as Social Security, unemployment compensation, public assistance), and other cash receipts (such as private pensions and alimony). It does not include capital gains, imputed rents, or government or private benefits provided in kind (such as food stamps, Medicare, and employer-provided health insurance), nor does it subtract taxes paid, although all of these affect a family's standard of living.

Time series data on a more comprehensive definition of income—money income plus noncash transfers minus direct federal taxes paid—have recently become available (for example, U.S. Bureau of the Census, 1992c), but only for the period after 1979. We analyze this more comprehensive measure in our discussion of the trend in poverty, but in order to study a consistent record for the past four decades, we limit our microdata analyses to the Census Bureau's definition of money income.

Defining Families.   The Census defines a family as "a group of two or more persons related by birth, marriage or adoption and residing together." Not all persons, of course, live in families. Census Bureau reports on family incomes exclude unrelated individuals, defined as "persons who are not living with any relatives." In 1991 there were 36.8 million unrelated individuals whose incomes were not included in the published data, and 67.2 million families whose incomes were counted. Thus, for every two households whose incomes were included, about one household was ignored. In 1960, when unrelated individuals made up a much smaller proportion of all households, only one unrelated individual was ignored for every four families included. Because the Census has always gathered income data consistently for both families and unrelated individuals, however, we can incorporate information on all persons in the population into our analyses. Doing so affects both levels and trends in family income.

In recent years the Census Bureau has published a time series on households. Households are defined to include unrelated individuals as well as families. Because these data are not widely cited, we do not report them in this book. In our microeconomic analyses we include families and unrelated individuals in a manner that is similar to the Bureau's "household" concept: we count each unrelated individual as a family of one person.

Our measure of income-sharing units differs from the Census concept of the household in that the Census Bureau sums the incomes of all individuals who share a residence, while we sum only the incomes of related persons. For example, if a family of four has a lodger renting a room in its household, the Census will count the residence as a household of five persons. We record one four-person family and one one-person family. We implicitly assume that unrelated people do not share income, even if they reside at the same address.

The Census household measure is more appropriate for a living arrangement that has become more common in recent years—cohabiting unmarried couples. Unfortunately, the CPS does not ask questions that make it possible to distinguish cohabiting couples from roommates. Thus we count such a couple as two unrelated individuals and treat their incomes as separate, while the Census counts them as a two-person household and sums their incomes. The 1990 Census allows one to treat cohabiting couples as if they were married couples. Our analysis of those data shows that treating cohabitors as married couples would have almost no effect on the trends we discuss.

Defining Race and Ethnicity. In our empirical work, we classify all persons into four mutually exclusive racial/ethnic groups—white non-Hispanics, black non-Hispanics, Hispanics, and other races. The last group includes Native Americans, Asian-Americans, Pacific Islanders, and others; these make up such a small percentage of the total population that sample sizes in the Current Population Survey are too small for us to reliably estimate their group-specific measures of poverty and mean living standards. Therefore, in Chapter 4 we report results only for the first three groups. All persons, regardless of race or ethnicity, are included in all of our other analyses.

Our classification differs from the one used by the Bureau of the Census in its publications. The Bureau reports categories that are not mutually exclusive—whites, blacks, and Hispanics, with Hispanics double-counted in the first two categories.

The quality of information by which we identify Hispanics has varied over time. We used the best information available in any year. In the 1950 Census we used "Spanish surname," which clearly yields an underestimate. In the 1970 Census the household head was asked if she or he was of Hispanic origin. Sample sizes are also too small for us to effectively decompose the Hispanic population into its various subgroups, such as those whose origin was Mexico, Puerto Rico, Cuba, and so on.

Adjusting for Inflation. Problems arose with the consumer price index (CPI-U) in the 1970s, because of the way it reflected changes in the costs of home ownership. This was a period of rising home prices and interest rates, and the measure gave too much weight to the costs of owning a home. This produced an overstatement of inflation. As a result, a new price index, the CPI-U-X1, was adopted in 1983. It is less affected by housing prices and mortgage interest rates because it estimates the cost of renting and not purchasing a home. Use of the CPI-U thus overstates inflation and understates income growth during the period when income growth slowed. For example, between 1973 and 1982, the CPI-U rose by 117 percent, while the CPI-U-X1 rose by 103 percent. Real median income fell by 10.5 percent, if the CPI-U is used to measure inflation, while it fell by 4 percent if the CPI-U-X1 is used. We incorporate the CPI-U-X1 as far back as 1968 in our analyses. Thus, even though the data in Table 3.1 are derived from published Census Bureau reports, they differ from the "official" published data, which incorporate the CPI-U-X1 only after 1983.

Measuring Poverty. Ruggles (1990) argues that the official poverty lines, based on research by Mollie Orshansky (1963, 1965), reflected an appropriate absolute minimum standard of living thirty years ago, but not today. She proposes an updated poverty threshold based not just on the costs of purchasing a necessary amount of food but on the costs of purchasing a broader number of necessities. She would reevaluate the poverty threshold based on the costs of these necessities every decade to reflect changes in society's notion of a minimum standard of living. Ruggles suggests several alternative poverty lines, including one that incorporates a minimum standard of housing consumption and one that updates the Orshansky method by using more recent family budgets and food shares.

As we noted in Chapter 3, our measurement of poverty is based on the official poverty line and is thus conservative. Still, poverty rates that use the official line are found by most observers to be higher than anticipated. Following Ruggles's proposals would mean an even higher rate of poverty.

To measure poverty, the federal government compares a family's or an individual's money income during a calendar year with an official income threshold. If a family's total money income during the calendar year falls below this threshold, then all persons in the family are classified as poor. These thresholds are adjusted for family size, age of the head of the family, and number of children under age 18. Until 1981 there were separate poverty lines for farm and nonfarm families and for families headed by men and those headed by women. The rationales for these differences were that farm families were assumed to grow some of their own food and that men and women need different amounts of food. The cutoffs provide an "absolute" measure of poverty that specifies the income necessary to provide minimally decent levels of consumption. For 1991 they ranged from $6,532 for a single person over age 65 to $27,942 for a family of nine or more persons. The average threshold for a family of four was $13,924.

The equivalence scales implicit in the poverty line were originally developed by Mollie Orshansky (1963, 1965) from information on dietary intake, and therefore reflect economies of scale in food consumption, not economies of scale measured over all consumer goods. If per capita income had been chosen as an equivalence scale, then a family of four (two adults and two children) would have a poverty line twice as large as that of a nonelderly couple. The official poverty line is based on the assumption that children consume less than adults. As a result, the official poverty line for this family of four is 1.51 times that of the couple. Likewise, the poverty line for an elderly couple would be the same as that for a nonelderly couple if per capita income were used. The official line, however, is based on the finding that the elderly require less food than younger people, so the poverty line for an elderly couple is 0.9 times that of the nonelderly couple. Ruggles (1990) argues that this equivalence scale is no longer appropriate for the elderly, and that if the scales were based on a broader range of consumption items rather than on food alone, the line for the elderly would not be lower than that for younger people.

The official poverty cutoffs are updated yearly by an amount corresponding to the change in the consumer price index so that they represent the same purchasing power each year. This means that the poverty line for a family of four of $13,924 in 1991 should buy the same consumption goods as the comparable line of $2,973 in 1959—the full difference should reflect increases in prices, and not a rising standard of living.

As we have mentioned, poverty lines based on the CPI-U-X1 better reflect changes in prices. The poverty threshold for a family of four in 1991 according to this measure was $12,667. We use the CPI-U-X1 poverty line from 1968 onward. Thus our analysis of rising poverty yields a more conservative estimate than would have been the case if we had used the official measure.

The use of an *absolute* poverty line—one that is adjusted only for inflation and does not change as real income changes—means that the poverty line falls further behind the average living standard during periods of economic growth. In contrast, a *relative* poverty measure is defined in some fixed relationship to the standard of living, for example, 50 percent of the median. In 1959 a nonfarm family of four at the poverty line had an income that was 55 percent as large as the median family income. Because real median family income grew over the next fifteen years, this ratio fell to 38 percent by 1973. Because income growth has been so slow over the past two decades, it was also about 38 percent in 1991. If the official poverty concept were a relative one, however, the current poverty line, and hence the poverty rate, would be substantially higher (see Danziger, Haveman, and Plotnick, 1986, for a discussion of the trend in a relative poverty measure). We use the official poverty line to measure absolute changes in the well-being of those at the bottom of the income distribution and measures of inequality to determine how those at the bottom are faring relative to the rest of the population.

Notes

1. The Diminishing American Dream

1. The official poverty line for a family of four in 1973 was $4,550, which is equivalent, after adjustment for inflation, to $13,924 in 1991. College graduates do fare much better than high school graduates: 30 percent of male and 57 percent of female high school graduates between the ages of 25 and 34 earned less than $13,924 in 1991.
2. The baseline is 100, the average for 1966. A reading of 95 means that the confidence level during the 1950s and 1960s averaged about 5 percent below the 1966 level. Confidence in the 1980s was thus about 20 percent below that level. For the early 1990s the index has averaged 72. It was 82.7 in April 1994.
3. That the rich fared so well in the market economy of the 1980s, at the same time that their income tax rates were cut so much, does have important implications for raising the revenue to fund the policy agenda we propose in Chapter 8.

2. Public Policies since the War on Poverty

1. At that time the poverty gap—the difference between a family's income and its poverty line summed over all poor persons—was about $11 billion (or about $46 billion in 1991 constant dollars). The poverty gap in 1991 was about $66 billion.
2. The Food Stamp Act of 1964 initially authorized a three-year program to provide better food for the poor. The number of people receiving food stamps grew from fewer than 1 million in 1964 to more than 25 million in the 1990s. See MacDonald (1977) for an early history and analysis of the program.

3. Many of the programs introduced or expanded during the War on Poverty–Great Society era are still in place. And, despite budget cutbacks in the 1980s, spending on these programs increased to 12.9 percent of GNP by 1992. If Social Security, Medicare, Medicaid, and other medical assistance are excluded, however, social welfare spending fell from 4.3 percent to 3.8 percent of GNP between 1975 and 1992 (Burtless, 1994).

4. Because the official poverty line is indexed for inflation, it increases each year. Over this period, however, the standard deduction and personal exemptions were fixed.

5. For a historical review of social welfare spending, see Falk et al. (1993).

6. A family can receive the EITC only by filing a tax return. When the EITC was first introduced it was thought of as offsetting the Social Security tax payments of the working poor.

7. In 1994 the EITC credit rate was 7.65 percent for workers without children, 26.3 percent for workers with one child, and 30 percent for workers with two or more children (Scholz, 1994).

8. David Ellwood (1988), in an influential work that reflected this new consensus, proposed converting welfare into a transitional system providing cash support for up to three years, supplemented by government provision of minimum-wage jobs and guaranteed child support. These proposals formed the basis for President Clinton's welfare reform proposals, the Work and Responsibility Act of 1994.

9. Of the $1 billion in 1990 federal matching funds available for state programs sponsored under the FSA, only $684 million was used (Heclo, 1994). Also, the states have assigned a very small percentage of JOBS participants to subsidized work programs, in part because of the expense of such programs (Levitan and Gallo, 1993).

10. This represents an increase of about $650 for a family of four.

11. Full-time, full-year work at the 1994 minimum wage of $4.25 yielded an annual income of $8,500. The 1994 official poverty lines for families of three and four persons were $11,849 and $15,192.

12. President Carter's Program for Better Jobs and Income proposed both to make cash welfare universally available and to provide minimum-wage public service jobs for adults with children who were expected to work but who could not find regular private- or public-sector jobs.

3. Trends in the Level and Distribution of Income

1. Problems arose with the CPI-U in the 1970s, and as a result the Census Bureau adopted a new price index, the CPI-U-X1, in 1983. For

the difference between the two measures, see "A Note on the Data," page 177. We incorporate the CPI-U-X1 as far back as 1968 in Table 3.1. Thus while the data in Table 3.1 are all derived from published Census reports, they differ from the "official" published data, which incorporate the CPI-U-X1 only after 1983.

2. Figure 3.1 indexes both the mean and the median at 1.0 in 1947. The index values after 1947 are adjusted for inflation. Any year's deviation from 1.0 shows the percentage change between that year's income and the 1947 level. By 1973, for example, the index for the median was 2.04 and that for the mean was 1.97. Thus in 1973 the median was 104 percent higher than in 1947; the mean, 97 percent higher.

3. The postwar recessions are listed by the National Bureau of Economic Research as follows: eleven months, November 1948–October 1949; ten months, July 1953–May 1954; eight months, August 1957–April 1958; ten months, April 1960–February 1961; eleven months, December 1969–November 1970; sixteen months, November 1973–March 1975; six months, January–July 1980; sixteen months, July 1981–November 1982; and nine months, July 1990–March 1991.

4. Measured by annual growth in the mean, the recovery of the 1980s was roughly two-thirds as rapid as the expansion of the 1960s; measured by growth in the median, it was only half the rate of the 1960s recovery.

5. If unrelated individuals are counted as families of one person, mean family size fell from 3.1 in 1950 to 2.8 in 1973 to 2.4 in 1989. This decline is relevant to our microdata analyses, which analyze all income-sharing units, families, and unrelated individuals.

6. The series shown in column 1 of Table 3.2 is based on Census Bureau concepts. We use data from the 1950, 1960, and 1970 censuses for the early years; CPS microdata are not consistently available for years before 1967. Also, the measurement procedures in the CPS and the Census are somewhat different, so we never mix the two sources of data in measuring a trend. Although the postwar boom extended from 1947 to 1973, we proxy that period with the 1949–1969 comparison of census data.

7. While the two concepts are obviously related, poverty and inequality may move in opposite directions. For example, if everyone's income grows rapidly but the incomes of the rich grow fastest, then poverty will fall but inequality will rise. Similarly, if everyone's income falls during a recession but the incomes of the rich fall most, then poverty will rise but inequality will fall.

8. The mean incomes of families in the bottom and top quintiles differ

from the incomes of those at the 20th and 80th percentiles. The income of a family at the 20th percentile will be higher than the average income of the bottom quintile, as the latter is the average of all family incomes up to the 20th percentile. Similarly, families at the 80th percentile have the lowest incomes in the top quintile.

9. The Tax Reform Act of 1986 and the Omnibus Reconciliation Act of 1990 did make some progressive changes, notably an expansion of the Earned Income Tax Credit. Nonetheless, federal income and payroll taxes were less progressive in 1990 than a decade earlier. For a discussion of changes in tax policy, see Chapters 2 and 7.

10. In earlier work (Danziger, Gottschalk, and Smolensky, 1989) we defined the rich as those whose incomes were above nine times the poverty line over the period 1973–1987. For this book we use seven times the poverty line because we have extended our series back to 1949, when far fewer persons were "rich."

11. As in Ross, Danziger, and Smolensky (1987), we extend the official poverty measure back to 1949 using the CPI.

12. A series that adjusted for in-kind income and taxes would show a larger decline in poverty than the official series from the mid-1960s to the mid-1970s, the period during which in-kind transfers grew very rapidly.

13. The adjustments reflected in columns 2–4 of Table 3.5 lower the official poverty rate by reducing the poverty threshold and including in-kind transfers. In addition, certain types of income are underreported to the Census Bureau. To the extent that the poor underreport their incomes, the official poverty rate is overstated.

14. This aggregate story does not fit the experience of all demographic groups. For example, children have fared worse than average and the elderly better than average over the past two decades; see Chapter 4.

4. Demographic Groups with Persisting Disadvantages

1. The average hourly earnings of production or nonsupervisory workers in private nonagricultural industries, including part-time as well as full-time and male as well as female workers, were (in constant 1992 dollars) $7.77 in 1949, $10.83 in 1969, $11.71 in 1973, and $10.65 in 1991. Bosworth and Perry (1994), reviewing measures of real compensation that include employer-paid fringe benefits and taxes, find that all grew by less than one percent per year between 1973 and 1993. For more detailed discussion of changes in men's real wages since the 1960s, see Chapter 6.

2. See Gottschalk and Mayer (1994) for a discussion of the offsetting de-

crease in home production that accompanied the increase in the market work of wives.

3. In this chapter we review trends in economic well-being for three groups classified by age and/or sex and three groups classified by race or ethnicity. In Chapter 5, where our focus is on the effect of demographic changes on overall measures of the level and distribution of income and poverty, we will distinguish twelve demographic groups.

4. Persons age 65 or over are classified as elderly. All married-couple families are classified as headed by males. Some of the elderly live in families headed by nonelderly persons; some of the nonelderly live in families headed by elderly persons. For example, if a 70-year-old widow moves into her adult son's home, she will be counted as living in a family headed by a nonelderly man. Similarly, if a married couple moves into the home of one spouse's elderly parents, they will be counted as living in a family headed by an elderly person. Classifying each person according to his or her own age and gender would make little difference to the themes we emphasize.

5. To measure a child's well-being, we divide total family income by the poverty line, which is a function of family size. For most of our analyses we then weight each family by the number of persons to get adjusted family income for each person. In this instance, however, we weight by the number of children to get adjusted family income for each child. The living standards of families with children tend to be lower than those of similar families without children because of the larger family size of the former; family income does not increase very much as family size increases.

6. Note that including Food Stamps, Medicaid, and other in-kind programs in the analysis would increase income and reduce poverty in all years. However, the decline in real in-kind benefits in the 1980s would decrease the growth rate of income and the reduction in poverty.

7. Male unrelated individuals and male heads of families not living with a spouse, by definition, do not have any earnings from a spouse; if the category were *married* nonelderly males, the percentage of family income attributable to wives' earnings would be higher.

8. For a discussion of explanations of long-term trends in the labor force participation rates of married women, see Goldin (1990). The major reasons include wider opportunities and higher wage rates for women, reduced numbers of children, increased probability of divorce, and changes in social norms. For a detailed analysis of changes in women's contribution to family income see Cancian, Danziger, and Gottschalk (1993a).

9. The data in Table 4.3 are for all persons living in families headed by

nonelderly women. Many of these families do not include children, and hence are not eligible for government programs such as Aid to Families with Dependent Children. We discuss the situation of female heads of families with children later on.

10. The amount of income provided by absent fathers is likely to be under-reported by the mothers in Census surveys, but there is no evidence that this underreporting has increased.

11. If the value of the benefits the elderly have received from Medicare and Medicaid since 1965 were to be included, their gains relative to those of the nonelderly and children would be even greater than those shown in the tables in this chapter.

12. Figure 4.2 includes as low earners both men who did not work during the year and those who worked but had low earnings. If the sample is restricted only to earners, the low earnings rate in every year is lower, but the trends are similar (see Danziger, 1991; Acs and Danziger, 1993). The poverty line is adjusted for inflation for each year and was $12,667 in 1991.

13. There is evidence of the existence of a growing inner-city minority underclass (Mincy, 1994). However, the underclass is small, roughly 2 percent of the population and 10 percent of the minority population. Its difficulties cannot account for the widespread economic hardship evident for all racial/ethnic groups.

14. Children are classified according to the race and sex of the head of their family. Thus they are classified as living in a male-headed family if they live with their father and mother, their father alone, or their grandfather or another male relative.

15. Recall that the value of Food Stamps and other noncash benefits is not included in our measure of poverty. Including them, however, would not reverse any of the differences by race/ethnicity or by age. For example, when noncash benefits are included and taxes excluded, 15.3 percent of children and 11.0 percent of the elderly were poor in 1991 (see U.S. House of Representatives, Committee on Ways and Means, 1993).

5. Why Poverty Remains High

1. See Tienda and Liang (1994) for a review of the causes of these changes.

2. When we implement this decomposition using multiple demographic groups, we use the overall growth in average income, not the group-specific growth. Throughout our analyses we use our measure of in-

come divided by the family's poverty line and weighted so as to count each person once.

3. We could use the observed Year 1 or Year 2 distribution of income instead of the simulated distribution; doing so would make a quantitative but not a qualitative difference in our results.

4. This calculation treats changes in poverty rates and changes in the demographic composition of the population as if they were independent of one another, and ignores any behavioral links between them. As an example of such a link, suppose the growing number of female-headed families (a demographic change) increases the AFDC caseload and that policymakers respond by reducing AFDC benefits, thus raising the poverty rate for female-headed families. Or suppose that falling wages and rising unemployment among men (economic changes) make them less likely to marry or to stay married, thus increasing the number of persons living in female-headed families.

5. The simulations in this chapter are based on poverty rates that differ slightly from those in Chapters 3 and 4 because of changes in computer software that were introduced while this book was being written. The tables in Chapters 3 and 4 show a decline of 25.2 percentage points in poverty between 1949 and 1969, whereas Table 5.3 shows a 25.7 point decline.

6. There is an interaction in our simulation because disadvantages are not simply additive; the interaction term appears in row 3c of the table. Both race and family structure, for instance, directly affect the poverty rate: blacks have a higher poverty rate than whites; female-headed families have a higher rate than male-headed families. Because of the interaction between race and family structure, the effect on the poverty rate of living in a family headed by a black woman may be smaller than the sum of the effects of living in a black family and living in a female-headed family. The negative interaction terms in row 3c of the table indicate that this is the case. Because our analysis is based on twelve demographic groups, there are multiple interactions whose sums may be positive (poverty-increasing) or negative (poverty-decreasing).

7. Blank and Card (1993), using a different methodology, find that labor market changes would have raised the poverty rate by 0.8 percentage points between 1979 and 1989. The economy grew faster between 1979 and 1989 than during the 1973–1991 period as a whole; most of the increased inequality over the longer period occurred in this decade.

8. Other recent studies have found demographic effects similar to this increase of one-tenth of a percentage point per year: Cutler and Katz (1991) found an increase of 2 to 3 points over twenty-six years; Blank

and Card (1993), an increase of 2.5 to 3.5 points over twenty-four years.

9. The coefficient of variation squared in year t can be written as follows:

$$cv^2 = S_1^2 cv_1^2 + S_2^2 cv_2^2 + S_3^2 cv_3^2$$

$$+ 2r_{12}S_1S_2cv_1^2cv_2^2 + 2r_{13}S_1S_3cv_1^2cv_3^2 + 2r_{32}S_3S_2cv_3^2cv_2^2$$

where cv_i^2 is the squared coefficient of variation of income source i, S_i is the share of family income coming from source i, and $r_{i,j}$ is the correlation between income sources i and j. The impact of changes in inequality of earnings is calculated by changing cv_1^2 from its initial-year value (e.g., 1949) to its subsequent-year value (e.g., 1969). The value of cv_2^2 is then changed to determine the impact of changes in inequality of the earnings of other family members. The residual category is calculated by changing all other terms in the identity, and therefore includes the effects of changes in inequality of the residual source (all income other than earnings) and changes in all income shares and correlations. While the order in which the terms are changed can affect the results, in practice our qualitative conclusions are not affected by order. For a detailed description of this decomposition technique see Cancian, Danziger, and Gottschalk (1993b).

10. We exclude persons in families headed by women and by the elderly because they are more dependent on government transfers, as shown in Chapter 4. Our goal here is to emphasize the role of labor market changes, which are the focus of Chapters 6 and 7.

11. While between 1949 and 1969 the mean of the male heads' earnings almost doubled and earnings inequality declined, between 1973 and 1991 the mean declined slightly and inequality increased. Thus there were major differences between the two periods in both earnings growth and earnings inequality.

6. Changes in Labor Markets

1. Increases in inequality of annual earnings could have come from changes in the distribution of hours rather than in the distribution of wage rates. However, using the March CPS, both Burtless (1993) and Moffitt (1990) find that changes in the distribution of hours could have explained, at best, a small part of the rise in inequality during the 1980s. Their analysis may suffer from the weakness of the wage measures in the March CPS. Karoly and Klerman (1991), using the May CPS, which has much better information on wages and hours, find a

strong upward trend in the dispersion of wage rates during the 1980s; they also assign a minor role to changes in hours.

2. Comparable data are not available for earlier years.

3. Bosworth and Perry (1994) argue that the divergence between real wages and productivity partially reflects differences in deflators used for the two series. When the same deflator is used for both series the two move closely together.

4. A worker at the 10th percentile earns more than 10 percent of the working population; the median worker is at the 50th percentile. We proxy low-wage workers by examining the 10th percentile and high-wage workers by the 90th percentile.

5. Part of this increase may reflect the fact that women worked more hours per week or that the new labor market entrants worked more hours and earned more per hour. These issues make it more difficult to interpret weekly wage data for women. Because men's changing hours of work are not likely to reflect voluntary changes in attachment to the labor force, we, and other researchers, emphasize changes in the level and distribution of men's earnings.

6. The decline in inequality between men and women and the differences between the two groups' patterns of inequality explain why Harrison and Bluestone (1988), who combine men and women, find a U-turn (falling then rising inequality). Studies that focus on men and women separately do not find a decline in inequality before 1975; for a review see Karoly (1993).

7. When comparing groups of workers by length of experience in the labor force, we approximate actual experience by calculating the number of years of potential experience following the last year of education. (For example, a 28-year-old high school graduate will have ten years of potential experience: age − education − 6 = experience.)

8. While the precise allocation of the change in inequality to changes within and between groups depends on the number of groups analyzed and the concept of earnings used, all studies show substantial increases in within-group inequality over the past two decades. The more narrowly defined the group, the more groups there will be, so the greater the share of total inequality that will be allocated to between-group inequality.

9. For comparisons between other countries and the United States, see Freeman and Needles, 1993 (Canada); Borland, 1992 (Australia); Katz and Loveman, 1990 (United Kingdom and France); Katz and Revenga, 1989 (Japan). Country-specific studies are also available for Australia (Saunders, Stott, and Hobbes, 1991), Germany (Abraham and House-

man, 1993), Italy (Erickson and Ichino, 1992), Korea (Kim and Topel, 1992), and Sweden (Hibbs, 1990; Edin and Holmlund, 1992).

10. This view was put forth in a study by the Office of Tax Analysis (OTA) of the U.S. Treasury Department (1992) during the 1992 presidential campaign. OTA argued that the rise in inequality had been largely offset by increased economic mobility. The study, however, confused changes in income over the life cycle with changes in mobility. OTA classified persons as economically mobile if their income increased with age, even if they stayed at the bottom of the distribution for their cohort. The Treasury report and the subsequent Urban Institute report (Sawhill and Condon, 1992) focused on mobility of total family income. Moffitt and Gottschalk (1993) focus on earnings mobility.

11. Higher mobility leads to lower inequality measured over long periods because it moderates differences in yearly earnings: for most individuals, good years will tend to be balanced by poor years.

12. Sawhill and Condon (1992) attribute this analogy to Joseph Schumpeter.

13. Some writers use the term economic mobility to describe changes in earnings over time for the *same* individual, defining a person with rising earnings as upwardly mobile even if the increase is not large enough to keep the person in the same position in the earnings distribution. In our usage, however, individuals are upwardly mobile only if their earnings rise relative to the earnings of those at higher levels of the distribution.

14. A focus on only the poorest or the richest workers tends to understate the amount of mobility since, by definition, those at the bottom can change positions only by moving up, while those at the top can only move down. In contrast, those in the middle of the distribution can move in either direction. More than 50 percent of those in the middle three quintiles changed positions between adjacent years.

15. Mishel and Bernstein (1994a) report a decline in mobility but their measure reflects the decline in mean wages.

7. Why Inequality of Earnings Increased

1. Of course, the size of the labor force can be changed in unforeseen ways by changes in immigration policy.

2. See Okun (1975) for a classic discussion of this tradeoff.

3. One of the textbook roles for government action is to offset adverse distributional changes brought about by market forces.

4. Their simulations included possible labor supply effects.

5. Freeman's accounting does not necessarily imply causation. Because it is possible that the decline in unionization was caused by the weakened demand for blue-collar workers, it is not possible to deduce whether the decline in unionization *caused* inequality to increase, or whether other labor market changes caused the rise in inequality, which *caused* the decline in unionization.

6. It is possible that poor economic conditions after the late 1970s partially countered the incentive effects of the cuts in real welfare benefits. However, an extensive experimental literature (see Burtless, 1986) indicates that the effects of government transfers on labor supply and family structure are much smaller than those required to confirm Murray's hypothesis.

7. For recent evidence, see Murnane, Willett, and Levy (1994). Of course, if test scores are not good measures of skills, then the trend in test scores does not provide a test of this hypothesis.

8. Smolensky et al. (1994) were the first to use this method of displaying the data.

9. This shift to a more educated labor force in all industries occurred in spite of the increased cost of hiring college graduates.

10. The sum of imports and exports as a percentage of GNP is a commonly used measure of the extent of foreign competition because both importers and exporters are affected by prices of the goods they buy or sell overseas.

11. Imports account for +.029 percent per year of the rise in the share of nonproduction workers (between industries). Exports account for an additional +.019. The total increase in the share is .552 percent per year. See also Haltiwanger and Davis (1991).

12. Capelli (1993) documents the upgrading of skill requirements for production workers during the 1980s—a full step increase on a seven-step job ladder (p. 524).

13. Data on productivity growth is, at best, a measure of the degree to which technology changed the ratio of outputs to some aggregate measure of all inputs. It does not provide evidence on the form of the technological change (i.e., whether or not it was skill-biased). The timing issue and the previously discussed measurement issue are not unrelated. Those who argue that technology must be directly observed—for example, Mishel and Bernstein (1994b)—cannot in turn argue that technology failed to accelerate during the 1980s. If technology, like Pluto, cannot be observed, then it is impossible to determine whether it accelerated or not.

14. Any link between part-time work and earnings instability requires both

that part-time workers have greater instability and that they comprise a growing proportion of the labor force (or that instability *among* part-timers rose even when their numbers were constant).

15. This decline is a result of declines in both the share of total employment in manufacturing and the probability that manufacturing workers would be laid off.

16. Increases in the use of temporary workers will also increase inequality of permanent earnings if the distribution of permanent earnings is less equal for temporary workers than for permanent workers with similar labor force characteristics.

17. According to the *Standard Industrial Classifications Manual*, the Help Services industry (SIC 7363) comprises establishments "supplying temporary or continuing help on a contract or fee basis. The help supplied is always on the payroll of the supplying establishments, but is under the direct or general supervision of the business to whom the help is furnished."

18. Even these figures probably understate its size. Carey and Hazelbaker (1986) speculate that the number may be 20 percent higher since many "job shops," which supply engineers and other technical personnel, are probably classified in the Engineering, Architectural, and Surveying Services industries (SIC 8911) rather than the Temporary Help industry. Also, Abraham (1990) estimates that workers employed by firms themselves, rather than through temporary help agencies, to do short-term work or to fill in when additional workers are needed may add another million temporary workers.

8. An Antipoverty Agenda

1. In fact, we do have a cash negative income tax—the Supplemental Security Income Program (SSI)—that provides a minimum annual income to the aged, blind, and disabled poor. And the Food Stamps program operates like an NIT, providing benefits in the form of coupons for food for all eligible poor persons.

2. If the rate of return is 10 percent, then it costs $10 in the current year to raise earnings in each future year by $1. For example, Heckman, Roselius, and Smith estimate that it would require an investment of about $25,000 for each male high school dropout and about $10,000 for each male high school graduate to raise their 1989 earnings in real terms back to the levels of 1979. This alone would cost $426 billion. The $1.7 trillion estimate is derived by considering all male and female workers without college degrees.

3. Topel (1994) has gone so far as to argue that *all* of the observed withdrawal from the labor force is a result of lower rewards to work. If this were the case, then policies that offset some of the declines in labor demand would have the indirect effect of drawing some of these potential workers back into the labor force.

4. We realize that our policy proposals do not address all aspects of the problem of poverty; for reforms that deal with the full range of the economic and family problems of the poor, see Danziger and Danziger (1993).

5. An analysis of labor market and antipoverty policies for the disabled or the elderly is beyond the scope of this book. For some, higher SSI or other transfer benefits might be appropriate. For others, programs that increase access to regular public- and private-sector jobs or that provide jobs for the disabled might be more appropriate. Such employment programs would be more expensive than the jobs of last resort that we discuss here.

6. Some of these families undoubtedly include persons other than the head who work part time but would prefer to work full time, full year, and who might also benefit from employment programs. Because of budget constraints, however, the public employment program we propose would be open to only one member of a family and would not be open to anyone living in nonpoor families.

7. Consider a young single mother whose only job opportunity paid the minimum wage and provided no medical insurance. In many states, her net income would be higher if she received welfare, which provides Medicaid coverage, than if she worked and paid for child care and medical insurance. If she chose this second option, she would appear in the "did not look for work" category, and we would not count her as a potential beneficiary of our policies. However, the provision of health insurance plus subsidized child care might induce her to enter the labor force and hence benefit from our proposals.

8. In 1993 a worker with one child received an EITC with a subsidy rate of 18.5 percent. The maximum EITC was $1,434 for a worker with one child who earned between $7,750 and $12,200, and $1,511 for a worker with two children who earned in this range. The EITC was phased down after earnings reached $12,200, so that it became zero at $23,050.

9. A full-time, full-year worker earning the minimum wage earns $8,500 in a year ($4.25 for 40 hours per week for 50 weeks). Thus minimum-wage workers with two or more children receive just about the maximum EITC.

10. This estimate was provided by David Betson, University of Notre Dame.
11. Sharon Parrott estimated the cost of this proposal using 1991 Current Population Survey data.
12. The official poverty line is based on pretax money income and is not adjusted for noncash benefits or work-related expenses, such as child care costs. We are evaluating this family's poverty status relative to its post-tax, post-transfer income, including food stamps and subtracting child care costs.
13. While two-parent families can be expected to have at least one full-time worker, many heads of one-parent families will be unable to work full time because of child care responsibilities. Additional policy reforms targeted on single-parent families are discussed below.
14. Ehrenberg (1992) reviews evidence suggesting that recent increases in the minimum wage have had modest effects on employment. Finegan and Burkhauser (1989) and Horrigan and Mincy (1993) document that they have had modest effects on poverty and inequality.
15. In two-earner families, the expenses claimed cannot exceed the earnings of the spouse with the lowest earnings.
16. In 1994 a single parent with one child began to owe federal income taxes at $10,500; a married couple with one child at $13,700.
17. This proposal is based on Robins (1990). To reduce the total cost of such a DCC expansion, the proposal could be phased out entirely for higher-income families, for example those with incomes above $75,000.
18. Michalopoulous, Robins, and Garfinkel (1992), using a behavioral model in which increased child care subsidies induce some mothers to work more and other mothers to shift from nonpaid to paid child care, estimate that implementing the Robins (1990) proposal would cost about three times this much.
19. One disadvantage of the tax credit approach is that phasing out the credits yields high cumulative tax rates for families with incomes between about $15,000 and $30,000.
20. The six states are Minnesota, Vermont, and Wisconsin, where the credit is refundable; and Iowa, Maryland, and Rhode Island, where it is not refundable but can be used to reduce tax payments. The thirty-six other states with income taxes could adopt a state EITC or a refundable daycare credit. The eight states that have no income tax, and thus could not adopt such refundable credits, also tend to impose the highest tax burdens on the poor. For more on state tax reform to help the poor, see McIntyre et al. (1991) and Hutchinson, Lav, and Greenstein (1992).
21. Bishop and Kang (1991) report that 28 percent of employers who had heard of the Targeted Jobs Tax Credit believed that subsidized workers

"make poorer new employees" than unsubsidized workers (7 percent thought subsidized workers make better workers). The percentage was even higher for employers who chose not to participate, implying that their low opinion of subsidized workers may have been a reason for their decision not to participate. Hollenbeck (1991) found that only nonwhite male youth benefited from the TJTC.

22. Displacement may also occur if the PSE workers provide public goods, such as cleaning of parks or supervision of public playgrounds, that are already provided by regular public-sector employees.

23. This assumes that our proposed EITC expansion for childless workers would be in place.

24. For example, in 1987 public expenditure on these programs was 0.01 percent of GDP in the United States, 0.10 in Australia, 0.02 in Canada, 0.06 in France, 0.10 in Japan, and 0.26 in Sweden. Implementing our PSE proposal would still leave U.S. total spending small relative to that of other countries (Layard and Nickell, 1991).

25. The origins of the President's plan to "end welfare as we know it" can be found in Ellwood (1988) and Bane and Ellwood (1994). Not coincidentally, Ellwood and Bane were Assistant Secretaries in the U.S. Department of Health and Human Services and two of the three co-chairs of the President's Task Force on Welfare Reform.

26. Because most absent parents are fathers, we use the terms "absent father" and "absent parent" interchangeably, while recognizing that increased child support should be expected of absent mothers as well.

27. CSAS would also reform the current judicial and administrative system for setting child support awards and collecting payments from absent parents. The obligation of the absent parent to support the child and the child's right to a minimum standard of living would be based on legislated guidelines and would thus be less affected by judicial discretion. Meyer et al. (1994) estimate that a child support reform of the type discussed here, with an assured benefit of $2,000 for the first child and $1,000 for each additional child, would have cost about $3 billion in 1985, or about $4.5 billion in the mid-1990s.

28. Absent parents would also benefit from our proposal to expand the EITC to childless workers, since most absent parents are "childless" for federal income tax purposes because their children do not live with them.

References

Aaron, Henry J. 1978. *Politics and the Professors: The Great Society in Perspective.* Washington, D.C.: Brookings Institution.

Abraham, Katharine G. 1990. "Restructuring the Employment Relationship: The Growth of Market-Mediated Work Arrangements." In *New Developments in the Labor Market: Toward a New Institutional Paradigm,* ed. Katharine G. Abraham and Robert B. McKersie, pp. 85–120. Cambridge, Mass.: M.I.T. Press.

Abraham, Katharine, and Susan E. Houseman. 1993. *Job Security in America: Lessons from Germany.* Washington, D.C.: Brookings Institution.

Acs, Gregory, and Sheldon H. Danziger. 1993. "Educational Attainment, Industrial Structure, and Male Earnings through the 1980s." *Journal of Human Resources* 28 (Summer): 618–648.

Anderson, Martin. 1990. "The Reagan Boom—Greatest Ever." *New York Times,* January 17.

Atkinson, Anthony B., François Bourguignon, and Christian Morrison. 1992. "Empirical Studies of Earnings Mobility." In *Fundamentals of Pure and Applied Economics,* ed. Jacques Lesourne and Hugo Sonnenschein, vol. 52. Philadelphia: Harwood Academic Publishers.

Bailey, Thomas. 1988. "Education and the Transformation of Markets and Technology in the Textile Industry." National Center on Education and Employment, Teachers College, Columbia University, Technical Paper no. 2.

Bane, Mary Jo, and David T. Ellwood. 1994. *Welfare Realities: From Rhetoric to Reform.* Cambridge, Mass.: Harvard University Press.

Barnow, Burt S. 1987. "The Impact of CETA Programs on Earnings: A Review of the Literature." *Journal of Human Resources* 22 (Spring): 157–193.

Bassi, Laurie, and Orley Ashenfelter. 1986. "The Effect of Direct Job Creation and Training Programs on Low-Skilled Workers." In Danziger and Weinberg, eds., 1986, pp. 133–151.

Bawden, D. Lee, ed. 1984. *The Social Contract Revisited: Aims and Outcomes of President Reagan's Social Welfare Policy*. Washington, D.C.: Urban Institute Press.

Belous, Richard S. 1989. *The Contingent Economy: The Growth of the Temporary, Part-Time and Subcontracted Workforce*. Washington, D.C.: National Planning Association.

Berman, Eli, John Bound, and Zvi Griliches. 1994. "Changes in the Demand for Skilled Labor within U.S. Manufacturing: Evidence from the Annual Survey of Manufacturers." *Quarterly Journal of Economics* 109 (May): 367–397.

Bishop, John H. 1989. "Toward More Valid Evaluations of Training Programs Serving the Disadvantaged." *Journal of Policy Analysis and Management* 8 (Spring): 209–228.

Bishop, John H., and Suk Kang. 1991. "Applying for Entitlements: Employers and the Targeted Jobs Tax Credit." *Journal of Policy Analysis and Management* 10 (Winter): 24–45.

Blank, Rebecca M. 1990. "Are Part-Time Jobs Bad Jobs?" In Burtless, ed., 1990, pp. 123–164.

——— 1993. "Why Were Poverty Rates So High in the 1980s?" In Papadimitriou and Wolff, eds., 1993, pp. 21–55.

Blank, Rebecca M., and Alan S. Blinder. 1986. "Macroeconomics, Income Distribution, and Poverty." In Danziger and Weinberg, eds., 1986, pp. 180–208.

Blank, Rebecca M., and David Card. 1993. "Poverty, Income Distribution, and Growth: Are They Still Connected?" *Brookings Papers on Economic Activity* 2: 285–339.

Blank, Rebecca, and Maria Hanratty. 1993. "Responding to Need: A Comparison of the Social Safety Net in Canada and the United States." In Card and Freeman, eds., 1993, pp. 191–232.

Blinder, Alan. 1980. "The Level and Distribution of Economic Well-Being." In *The American Economy in Transition*, ed. Martin Feldstein, pp. 415–499. Chicago: University of Chicago Press.

——— 1982. *The Truce in the War on Poverty: Where Do We Go from Here?* Washington, D.C.: National Policy Exchange, paper no. 3.

——— 1987. *Hard Heads, Soft Hearts: Tough-Minded Economics for a Just Society*. Reading, Mass.: Addison-Wesley.

Blinder, Alan S., and Howard Y. Esaki. 1978. "Macroeconomic Activity and Income Distribution in the Postwar United States." *Review of Economics and Statistics* 60: 604–609.

Bobo, Lawrence, and Ryan Smith. 1994. "Antipoverty Policy, Affirmative Action, and Racial Attitudes." In Danziger, Sandefur, and Weinberg, eds., 1994, pp. 365–395.

Borjas, George J., Richard B. Freeman, and Lawrence F. Katz. 1992. "On the Labor Market Effects of Immigration and Trade." In *Immigration and the Work Force: Economic Consequences for the United States and Source Areas*, ed. George J. Borjas and Richard B. Freeman. Chicago: University of Chicago Press.

Borland, Jeff. 1992. "Wage Inequality in Australia." Paper presented at National Bureau of Economic Research Conference, April.

Bosworth, Barry, and George L. Perry. 1994. "Productivity and Real Wages: Is There a Puzzle?" *Brookings Papers on Economic Activity* 1: 317–335.

Bound, John, and Richard Freeman. 1992. "What Went Wrong? The Erosion of Relative Earnings and Employment among Young Black Men in the 1980s." *Quarterly Journal of Economics* 107 (February): 201–232.

Bound, John, and George Johnson. 1992. "Changes in the Structure of Wages in the 1980s: An Evaluation of Alternative Explanations." *American Economic Review* 82 (3): 371–392.

Bumpass, Larry, and James Sweet. 1989. "Children's Experience in Single-Parent Families: Implications of Cohabitation and Marital Transitions." *Family Planning Perspectives* 21: 256–260.

Burt, Martha. 1992. *Over the Edge: The Growth of Homelessness in the 1980s*. New York: Russell Sage Foundation.

Burtless, Gary. 1986. "The Work Response to a Guaranteed Income: A Survey of Experimental Evidence." In *Lessons from the Income Maintenance Experiments*, ed. Alicia A. Munnell, pp. 22–52. Boston: Federal Reserve Bank.

———, ed. 1990. *A Future of Lousy Jobs? The Changing Structure of U.S. Wages*. Washington, D.C.: Brookings Institution.

——— 1993. "The Contribution of Employment and Hours Changes to Family Income Inequality." *American Economic Review* 83 (May): 131–135.

——— 1994. "Public Spending for the Poor: Historical Trends and Economic Limits." In Danziger, Sandefur, and Weinberg, eds., 1994, pp. 51–84.

Butler, Stuart, and Anna Kondratas. 1987. *Out of the Poverty Trap: A Conservative Strategy for Welfare Reform*. New York: Free Press.

Cancian, Maria, Sheldon H. Danziger, and Peter Gottschalk. 1993a. "The Changing Contributions of Men and Women to the Level and Distribution of Family Income, 1968–1988." In Papadimitriou and Wolff, eds., 1993, pp. 317–353.

———— 1993b. "Working Wives and Family Income Inequality among Married Couples." In Danziger and Gottschalk, eds., 1993, pp. 195–221.

Capelli, Peter. 1993. "Are Skill Requirements Rising? Evidence from Production and Clerical Jobs." *Industrial and Labor Relations Review* 46 (3): 515–529.

Card, David, and Richard Freeman, eds. 1993. *Small Differences That Matter: Labor Markets and Income Maintenance in Canada and the United States.* Chicago: University of Chicago Press.

Carey, Max L., and Kim L. Hazelbaker. 1986. "Employment Growth in the Temporary Help Industry." *Monthly Labor Review* (April): 37–44.

Caudill, Harry. 1963. *Night Comes to the Cumberlands: A Biography of a Depressed Area.* Boston: Little, Brown.

Chubb, John, and Paul Peterson, eds. 1985. *The New Direction in American Politics.* Washington, D.C.: Brookings Institution.

Clinton, Bill. 1992. *Putting People First: How We Can All Change America.* New York: Times Books.

Committee on Youth Employment Programs. 1985. *Youth Employment Programs: The YEDPA Years.* Washington, D.C.: National Academy Press.

Cutler, David M., and Lawrence F. Katz. 1991. "Macroeconomic Performance and the Disadvantaged." *Brookings Papers on Economic Activity* 2: 1–74.

Danziger, Sandra K., and Sheldon H. Danziger. 1993. "Child Poverty and Public Policy: Toward a Comprehensive Antipoverty Agenda." *Daedalus: America's Childhood* 122 (1): 57–84.

Danziger, Sheldon H. 1991. "The Poor." In *Human Capital and America's Future*, ed. David Hornbeck and Lester Salamon, pp. 139–167. Baltimore: Johns Hopkins University Press.

Danziger, Sheldon H., and Peter Gottschalk. 1985. "The Poverty of *Losing Ground*." *Challenge* (May–June): 32–38.

———— 1986. "Work, Poverty, and the Working Poor." *Monthly Labor Review* 109 (September): 17–26.

Danziger, Sheldon H., and Peter Gottschalk, eds. 1993. *Uneven Tides: Rising Inequality in America.* New York: Russell Sage Foundation.

Danziger, Sheldon H., Peter Gottschalk, and Eugene Smolensky. 1989. "How the Rich Have Fared, 1973–1987." *American Economic Review* 79 (May): 310–314.

Danziger, Sheldon H., Robert Haveman, and Robert Plotnick. 1986. "Antipoverty Policy: Effects on the Poor and Nonpoor." In Danziger and Weinberg, eds., 1986, pp. 50–77.

Danziger, Sheldon H., Gary D. Sandefur, and Daniel H. Weinberg, eds. 1994. *Confronting Poverty: Prescriptions for Change.* Cambridge, Mass.: Harvard University Press.

Danziger, Sheldon H., and Daniel H. Weinberg. 1994. "The Historical Record: Trends in Family Income, Inequality, and Poverty." In Danziger, Sandefur, and Weinberg, eds., 1994, pp. 18–50.

———, eds. 1986. *Fighting Poverty: What Works and What Doesn't.* Cambridge, Mass.: Harvard University Press.

Davis, Steven J. 1992. "Cross-Country Patterns of Change in Relative Wages." Working Paper no. 4085. Cambridge, Mass.: National Bureau of Economic Research.

Davis, Steven J., and Robert H. Topel. 1993. Comment on "International Trade and American Wages in the 1980s: Giant Sucking Sound or Small Hiccup?" by Robert Z. Lawrence and Matthew J. Slaughter. *Brookings Papers on Economic Activity: Microeconomics* 2: 214–221.

DiPrete, Thomas A. 1993. "Industrial Restructuring and the Mobility Response of American Workers in the 1980s." *American Sociological Review* 58: 74–96.

Duncan, Greg J., Timothy Smeeding, and Willard Rodgers. 1993. "Whither the Middle Class? A Dynamic View." In Papadimitriou and Wolff, eds., 1993, pp. 202–271.

Edin, Pers-Ander, and Bertil Holmlund. 1992. "The Swedish Wage Structure: The Rise and Fall of Solidaristic Wage Policy." Working Paper no. 13, Department of Economics, University of Uppsala.

Ehrenberg, Ronald. 1992. "New Minimum Wage Research: Symposium Introduction." *Industrial and Labor Relations Review* 26 (October): 3–5.

Ellwood, David. 1988. *Poor Support: Poverty in the American Family.* New York: Basic Books.

Ellwood, David, and Lawrence Summers. 1986. "Poverty in America: Is Welfare the Answer or the Problem?" In Danziger and Weinberg, eds., 1986, pp. 78–105.

Erickson, Christopher L., and Andrea C. Ichino. 1992. "Wage Differentials in Italy: Market Forces, Institutions, and Inflation." Paper presented at the National Bureau of Economic Research Conference, July.

Falk, Gene, Dawn Nuschler, and Richard Rimkunas. 1993. *1994 Budget Perspectives: Federal Spending for Social Welfare Programs.* CRS Report for Congress, 93–304 EPW. Washington, D.C.: Congressional Research Service.

Farber, Henry S. 1993. "The Incidence and Costs of Job Loss: 1982–91." *Brookings Papers on Economic Activity: Microeconomics*, pp. 73–132.

Feenberg, Daniel R., and James M. Poterba. 1992. "Income Inequality and the Incomes of Very High-Income Taxpayers: Evidence from Tax Returns." Working Paper no. 4229, December. Cambridge, Mass.: National Bureau of Economic Research.

Finegan, T. Aldrich, and Richard Burkhauser. 1989. "The Minimum Wage and the Poor: The End of a Relationship," *Journal of Policy Analysis and Management* 8 (Winter): 53–57.

Freeman, Richard B. 1992. "Crime and the Employment of Disadvantaged Youths." In *Urban Labor Markets and Job Opportunity*, ed. George E. Peterson and Wayne Vroman. Washington, D.C.: Urban Institute Press.

—— 1993. "How Much Has De-Unionization Contributed to the Rise in Male Earnings Inequality?" In Danziger and Gottschalk, eds., 1993, pp. 133–163.

Freeman, Richard B., ed. 1994. *Working under Different Rules*. New York: Russell Sage Foundation.

Freeman, Richard B., and Needles, Karen. 1993. "Skill Differentials in Canada in an Era of Rising Labor Market Inequality." In Card and Freeman, eds., 1993, pp. 45–67.

Galbraith, John Kenneth. 1958. *The Affluent Society*. New York: New American Library.

Garfinkel, Irwin. 1992. *Assuring Child Support: An Extension of Social Security*. New York: Russell Sage Foundation.

Garfinkel, Irwin, and Sara McLanahan. 1986. *Single Mothers and Their Children: A New American Dilemma*. Washington, D.C.: Urban Institute Press.

Glazer, Nathan. 1984. "The Social Policy of the Reagan Administration." In Bawden, ed., 1984.

Goldin, Claudia. 1990. *Understanding the Gender Gap: An Economic History of American Women*. Oxford: Oxford University Press.

Goldin, Claudia, and Robert A. Margo. 1992. "The Great Compression: The Wage Structure in the United States at Mid-Century." *Quarterly Journal of Economics* 107 (February): 1–34.

Goodwin, Doris Kearns. 1976. *Lyndon Johnson and the American Dream*. New York: Harper and Row.

Gottschalk, Peter. 1981. "Transfer Scenarios and Projections of Poverty into the 1980s." *Journal of Human Resources* 16 (Winter): 41–59.

—— 1994. "Policy Changes and Growing Earnings Inequality in Seven Industrialized Countries." Mimeo, Boston College, Department of Economics.

Gottschalk, Peter, and Sheldon H. Danziger. 1984. "Macroeconomic Conditions, Income Transfers, and the Trend in Poverty." In Bawden, ed., 1984, pp. 185–215.

—— 1985. "A Framework for Evaluating the Effects of Economic Growth and Transfers on Poverty." *American Economic Review* 75 (March): 153–161.

Gottschalk, Peter, Björn Gustafsson, and Edward Palmer. 1994. "What's behind the Increase in Inequality? An Introduction." Mimeo, Boston College, Department of Economics.

Gottschalk, Peter, and Mary Joyce. 1992. "Is Earnings Inequality Also Rising in Other Industrialized Countries?" Mimeo, Boston College, Department of Economics.

Gottschalk, Peter, Sara McLanahan, and Gary Sandefur. 1994. "The Dynamics and Intergenerational Transmission of Poverty and Welfare Participation." In Danziger, Sandefur, and Weinberg, eds., 1994, pp. 85–108.

Gottschalk, Peter, and Susan Mayer. 1994. "Changes in Home Production and Trends in Economic Inequality." Mimeo, Boston College, Department of Economics.

Gottschalk, Peter, and Robert Moffitt. 1994. "The Growth of Earnings Instability in the U.S. Labor Market." *Brookings Papers on Economic Activity* 2: 217–272.

Gramlich, Edward M., Richard Kasten, and Frank Sammartino. 1993. "Growing Inequality in the 1980s: The Role of Federal Taxes and Cash Transfers." In Danziger and Gottschalk, eds., 1993, pp. 225–249.

Green Book. See U.S. House of Representatives, Committee on Ways and Means.

Gueron, Judith, and Edward Pauly. 1991. *From Welfare to Work.* New York: Russell Sage Foundation.

Hahn, Andrew, and Robert Lerman. 1985. *What Works in Youth Employment Policy? How to Help Young Workers from Poor Families.* Washington, D.C.: National Planning Association.

Haltiwanger, John, and Steven J. Davis. 1991. "Wage Dispersion between and within U.S. Manufacturing Plants, 1963–86." *Brookings Papers on Economic Activity: Microeconomics*, pp. 115–200.

Hamermesh, Daniel S. 1989. "What Do We Know about Worker Displacement in the U.S.?" *Industrial Relations* 27 (Winter): 51–59.

Hanratty, Maria, and Rebecca Blank. 1992. "Down and Out in North America: Recent Trends in Poverty Rates in the United States and Canada." *Quarterly Journal of Economics* 107 (February): 233–254.

Harrington, Michael. 1962. *The Other America: Poverty in the United States.* New York: Macmillan.

Harrison, Bennett, and Barry Bluestone. 1988. *The Great U-Turn: Corporate Restructuring and the Polarizing of America.* New York: Basic Books.

Haveman, Robert H. 1988. *Starting Even: An Equal Opportunity Program to Combat the Nation's New Poverty.* New York: Simon and Schuster.

Heckman, James, Rebecca Roselius, and Jeffrey Smith. 1993. "U.S. Education and Training Policy: A Re-evaluation of the Underlying Assumptions behind the 'New Consensus.' " Mimeo, University of Chicago, Department of Economics.

Heclo, Hugh. 1986. "The Political Foundations of Antipoverty Policy." In Danziger and Weinberg, eds., 1986, pp. 312–340.

———— 1994. "Poverty Politics." In Danziger, Sandefur, and Weinberg, eds., 1994, pp. 396–437.

Hibbs, Douglas A., Jr. 1990. "Wage Dispersion and Trade Union Action in Sweden." In *Generating Equality in the Welfare State: The Swedish Experience*, ed. Inga Persson. Oslo: Norwegian University Press.

Hofferth, Sandra. 1995. "Caring for Children at the Poverty Line." *Children and Youth Services Review* 17 (1/2): 61–90.

Hollenbeck, Kevin. 1991. "Earnings Impact of the Targeted Jobs Tax Credit." Working Paper no. 91–07. Kalamazoo, Mich.: Upjohn Institute.

Hollister, Robinson, and Robert Haveman. 1991. "Direct Job Creation: Economic Evaluation and Lessons for the United States and Western Europe." In Anders Björklund et al., *Labour Market Policy and Unemployment Insurance*. New York: Oxford University Press.

Horrigan, Michael W., and Ronald B. Mincy. 1993. "The Minimum Wage and Earnings and Income Inequality." In Danziger and Gottschalk, eds., 1993, pp. 251–275.

Hungerford, Thomas I. 1993. "U.S. Income Mobility in the Seventies and Eighties." *Review of Income and Wealth*, ser. 39, no. 4 (December): 403–417.

Hutchinson, Frederick, Iris Lav, and Robert Greenstein. 1992. *A Hand Up: How State Earned Income Credits Help Working Families Escape Poverty.* Washington, D.C.: Center on Budget and Policy Priorities.

Jäntti, Markus, and Sheldon Danziger. 1994. "Child Poverty in Sweden and the United States: The Effect of Social Transfers and Parental Labor Force Participation." *Industrial and Labor Relations Review* 48 (October): 48–64.

Jaynes, Gerald, and Robin Williams, eds. 1989. *A Common Destiny: Blacks and American Society.* Washington, D.C.: National Academy Press.

Jenkins, Stephen. 1991. "Recent Trends in UK Income Inequality." In *Research on Economic Inequality*, ed. Daniel Slöttje. Greenwich, Conn.: JAI Press.

Johnson, Dirk. 1994. "Family Struggles to Make Do after Fall from Middle Class." *New York Times*, March 11.

Johnson, George. 1978. "Structural Unemployment Consequences of Job Creation Policies." In *Creating Jobs: Public Employment Programs and Wage Subsidies*, ed. John L. Palmer. Washington, D.C.: Brookings Institution.

Johnson, President Lyndon. 1964. "Letter of Transmittal." In *The Economic Report of the President*. Washington, D.C.: GPO.

Juhn, Chinhui, Kevin M. Murphy, and Brooks Pierce. 1993. "Wage Inequality and the Rise in the Returns to Skill." *Journal of Political Economy* 101 (June): 410–442.

Karoly, Lynn A. 1992. "Changes in the Distribution of Individual Earnings in the United States: 1967–1986." *Review of Economics and Statistics* 74 (1): 107–115.

———— 1993. "The Trend in Income Inequality among Families, Individuals, and Workers in the United States: A Twenty-Five-Year Perspective." In Danziger and Gottschalk, eds., 1993, pp. 19–97.

Karoly, Lynn A., and Jacob Alex Klerman. 1991. "Regional Differences in Increasing Earnings Inequality." Paper presented at the Population Association of America Annual Meetings, March.

Katz, Lawrence F., and Gary W. Loveman. 1990. "An International Comparison of Changes in the Structure of Wages: France, the United Kingdom, and the United States." Draft, Harvard University, Department of Economics.

Katz, Lawrence F., and Kevin M. Murphy. 1992. "Changes in Relative Wages, 1963–1987: Supply and Demand Factors." *Quarterly Journal of Economics* 107 (February): 35–78.

Katz, Lawrence F., and Ana L. Revenga. 1989. "Changes in the Structure of Wages: The U.S. vs. Japan." *Journal of Japanese and International Economics* (December): 522–553.

Kim, Dae-Il, and Robert H. Topel. 1992. "Labor Markets and Economic Growth: Lessons from Korea's Industrialization, 1970–1990." Paper presented at the National Bureau of Economic Research Conference, July.

Krueger, Alan B. 1993. "How Computers Have Changed the Wage Structure: Evidence from Microdata, 1984–89." *Quarterly Journal of Economics* 108 (February): 33–60.

Lampman, Robert. 1959. *The Low Income Population and Economic Growth*. U.S. Congress, Joint Economic Committee, Study Paper no. 12. Washington, D.C.: GPO.

———— 1971. *Ends and Means of Reducing Income Poverty*. Chicago: Markham.

———— 1974. "What Does It Do for the Poor? A New Test for National Policy." *Public Interest* 34 (Winter): 66–82.

Lawrence, Robert Z., and Matthew Slaughter. 1993. "International Trade and American Wages in the 1980s: Giant Sucking Sound or Small Hiccup?" *Brookings Papers on Economic Activity: Microeconomics* 2: 161– 226.

Layard, P. Richard, and Stephen J. Nickell. 1991. *Unemployment: Macro-*

economic Performance and the Labour Market. New York: Oxford University Press.

Lehman, Jeffrey. 1994. "Updating Urban Policy." In Danziger, Sandefur, and Weinberg, eds., 1994, pp. 226–252.

Lehman, Jeffrey, and Sheldon H. Danziger. 1995. "Ending Welfare as We Know It: Problems and Prospects." *Domestic Affairs*.

Lerman, Robert I. 1988. "Nonwelfare Approaches to Helping the Poor." *Focus* 11, no. 1 (Spring). University of Wisconsin–Madison, Institute for Research on Poverty.

Levitan, Sar, and Frank Gallo. 1993. "Jobs for JOBS: Toward a Work-Based Welfare System." Center for Social Policy Studies, George Washington University, Paper 1993–1.

Levitan, Sar, and Robert Taggart. 1976. *The Promise of Greatness*. Cambridge, Mass.: Harvard University Press.

Levy, Frank. 1987. *Dollars and Dreams: The Changing American Income Distribution*. New York: Russell Sage Foundation.

——— 1995. "Incomes and Income Inequality." In *State of the Union: America in the 1990s*, ed. Reynolds Farley, pp. 1–57. New York: Russell Sage Foundation.

Levy, Frank, and Richard J. Murnane. 1992. "U.S. Earnings Levels and Earnings Inequality: A Review of Recent Trends and Proposed Explanations." *Journal of Economic Literature* 30 (September): 1333–1381.

Lewin, Tamar. 1994. "Low Pay and Closed Doors Greet Young in Job Market." *New York Times*, March 10.

MacDonald, Maurice. 1977. *Food, Stamps, and Income Maintenance*. New York: Academic Press.

McIntyre, Robert S., M. P. Ettinger, D. P. Kelly, and E. A. Fray. 1991. *A Far Cry from Fair: CTJ's Guide to State Tax Reform*. Washington, D.C.: Citizens for Tax Justice.

Magnet, Myron. 1993. *The Dream and the Nightmare: The Sixties' Legacy to the Underclass*. New York: William Morrow.

Mead, Lawrence. 1992. *The New Politics of Poverty: The Working Poor in America*. New York: Basic Books.

Medoff, James L. 1993. "Middle-Aged and Out-of-Work: Growing Unemployment Due to Job Loss among Middle-Aged Americans." Democratic Study Center Report Series, April.

Melendez, Edwin. 1992. "Understanding Latino Poverty." *Hispanic Journal of Behavioral Sciences* 14, no. 1 (February): 4–15.

Meyer, Daniel R., Irwin Garfinkel, Donald Oellerich, and Philip Robins. 1994. "Who Should Be Eligible for an Assured Child Support Benefit?" In *Child Support and Child Well-Being*, ed. Irwin Garfinkel, Sara

McLanahan, and Philip Robins, pp. 175–205. Washington, D.C.: Urban Institute Press.

Michalopoulous, Charles, Philip Robins, and Irwin Garfinkel. 1992. "A Structural Model of Labor Supply and Child Care Demand." *Journal of Human Resources* 27 (Winter): 166–203.

Mincy, Ronald B., ed. 1994. *Nurturing Young Black Males: Challenges to Agencies, Programs, and Social Policy*. Washington, D.C.: Urban Institute Press.

Mirengoff, William, Lester Rindler, Harry Greenspan, and Scott Seablom. 1980. *CETA: Assessment of Public Service Employment Programs*. Washington, D.C.: National Academy of Sciences.

Mishel, Lawrence, and Jared Bernstein. 1994a. *The State of Working America, 1994–95*. Washington, D.C.: Economic Policy Institute.

———— 1994b. "Is the Technology Black Box Empty?: An Empirical Examination of the Impact of Technology on Wage Inequality and the Employment Structure." Washington, D.C.: Economic Policy Institute.

Moffitt, Robert. 1990. "The Distribution of Earnings and the Welfare State." In Burtless, ed., 1990, pp. 201–230.

Moffitt, Robert, and Peter Gottschalk. 1993. "Trends in the Covariance Structure of Earnings in the United States: 1969–1987." University of Wisconsin–Madison, Institute for Research on Poverty Discussion Paper no. 1001–1093, April.

Moss, Philip, and Chris Tilly. 1992. *Why Black Men Are Doing Worse in the Labor Market: A Review of Supply-Side and Demand-Side Explanations*. New York: Social Science Research Council.

Murnane, Richard J., John B. Willett, and Frank Levy. 1994. "The Growing Importance of Cognitive Skills in Wage Determination." Mimeo, Harvard University Graduate School of Education.

Murphy, Kevin, and Finis Welch. 1993. "Industrial Change and the Rising Importance of Skill." In Danziger and Gottschalk, eds., 1993, pp. 101–132.

Murray, Charles. 1984. *Losing Ground: American Social Policy, 1950–1980*. New York: Basic Books.

National Association of Temporary Services. 1993. "Temporary Help Industry Continues to Lead Employment Recovery." Press release, June.

National Commission on Children. 1991. *Beyond Rhetoric: A New Agenda for Children and Families*. Washington, D.C.: GPO.

Oellerich, Donald T., Irwin Garfinkel, and Philip Robins. 1991. "Private Child Support: Current and Potential Impacts." *Journal of Sociology and Social Welfare* 18 (1): 3–23.

Okun, Arthur M. 1975. *Equality and Efficiency: The Big Tradeoff*. Washington, D.C.: Brookings Institution.

Orshansky, Mollie. 1963. "Children of the Poor." *Social Security Bulletin* 26 (July): 3–13.

———— 1965. "Counting the Poor." *Social Security Bulletin* 28 (January): 3–29.

Palmer, John L., and Isabel V. Sawhill, eds. 1984. *The Reagan Record*. Cambridge, Mass.: Ballinger.

Papadimitriou, Dimitri B., and Edward N. Wolff, eds. 1993. *Poverty and Prosperity in the USA in the Late Twentieth Century*. London: Macmillan.

Peterson, Paul. 1985. "The New Politics of Deficits." In Chubb and Peterson, eds., 1985.

Phelps, Edmund. 1994. "Low-wage Employment Subsidies v. the Welfare State." *American Economic Review* 84 (May): 54–58.

Phillips, Kevin. 1990. *The Politics of Rich and Poor: Wealth and the American Electorate in the Reagan Aftermath*. New York: Random House.

Primus, Wendell E. 1989. "Children in Poverty: A Committee Prepares for an Informed Debate." *Journal of Policy Analysis and Management* 8 (Winter): 23–34.

Reagan, Ronald. 1986. Radio address. February 15.

Robins, Philip. 1990. "Federal Financing of Child Care: Alternative Approaches and Economic Implications." *Population Research and Policy Review* 9 (1): 65–90.

Ross, Christine, Sheldon H. Danziger, and Eugene Smolensky. 1987. "The Level and Trend of Poverty in the United States, 1939–1979." *Demography* 24 (November): 587–600.

Ruggles, Patricia. 1990. *Drawing the Line: Alternative Poverty Measures and Their Implications for Public Policy*. Washington, D.C.: Urban Institute Press.

Saunders, Peter, Helen Stott, and Gary Hobbes. 1991. "Income Inequality in Australia and New Zealand: International Comparisons and Recent Trends." *Review of Income and Wealth* 37 (March): 63–79.

Sawhill, Isabel, and Mark Condon. 1992. "Is U.S. Income Inequality Really Growing?" *Policy Bits*, no. 13. Washington, D.C.: Urban Institute.

Schlesinger, Arthur Meier. 1967. *A Thousand Days: John F. Kennedy in the White House*. Greenwich, Conn.: Fawcett.

Scholz, John K. 1994. "Tax Policy and the Working Poor: The Earned Income Tax Credit." *Focus* 15, no. 3. University of Wisconsin–Madison, Institute for Research on Poverty.

Shapiro, Isaac. 1988. *No Escape: The Minimum Wage and Poverty*. Washington, D.C.: Center on Budget and Policy Priorities.

Smeeding, Timothy. 1992. "Why the U.S. Antipoverty System Doesn't Work Very Well." *Challenge* 35 (January/February): 30–35.

Smolensky, Eugene, Sheldon H. Danziger, and Peter Gottschalk. 1988. "The Declining Significance of Age in the United States: Trends in the Well-Being of Children and the Elderly since 1939." In *The Vulnerable*, ed. John Palmer, Timothy Smeeding, and Barbara Torrey, pp. 29–54. Washington, D.C.: Urban Institute Press.

Smolensky, Eugene, Robert Plotnick, Erik Evenhouse, and Siobhan Reilly. 1994. "Growth, Inequality and Poverty: A Cautionary Tale." *Review of Income and Wealth* 40 (June): 217–222.

Steffick, Diane, and Linda Giannarelli. 1993. "Results of TRIM2 Simulations of a Refundable Child Care Tax Credit." Memo, Urban Institute, November 11.

Steuerle, Eugene. 1991. *The Tax Decade: How Taxes Came to Dominate the Public Agenda*. Washington, D.C.: Urban Institute Press.

Tienda, Marta, and Zai Liang. 1994. "Poverty and Immigration in Policy Perspective." In Danziger, Sandefur, and Weinstein, eds., 1994, pp. 330–364.

Tobin, James. 1967. "It Can Be Done! Conquering Poverty in the U.S. by 1976." *New Republic*. June 3, pp. 14–18.

––––––– 1970. "Raising the Incomes of the Poor." In *Agenda for the Nation*, ed. Kermit Gordon. Washington, D.C.: Brookings Institution.

Topel, Robert. 1994. "Regional Labor Markets and the Determinants of Wage Inequality." *American Economic Review* 84 (May).

Troy, Leo, and Neil Scheffrin. 1985. *Union Sourcebook*. West Orange, N.J.: IRDIS.

Uchitelle, Louis. 1993. "Thirty Years of Dwindling Hope for Prosperity." *New York Times*, May 6.

––––––– 1994. "Male, Educated, and in a Pay Bind." *New York Times*, February 11.

U.S. Bureau of the Census. 1976. *Historical Statistics, Colonial Times to the Present*. Washington, D.C.: GPO.

––––––– 1991a. *Statistical Abstract of the United States: 1991*. Washington, D.C.: GPO.

––––––– 1991b. *Poverty in the United States: 1990*. Current Population Reports, ser. P-60, no. 181. Washington, D.C.: GPO.

––––––– 1992a. *Money Income of Households, Families, and Persons: 1991*. Current Population Reports, ser. P-60, no. 180, August. Washington, D.C.: GPO.

––––––– 1992b. *Workers with Low Earnings: 1964 to 1990*. Current Population Reports, ser. P-60, no. 178. Washington, D.C.: GPO.

––––––– 1992c. *Measuring the Effects of Benefits and Taxes on Income and Poverty: 1979–1991*. Current Population Reports, ser. P-60, no. 182. Washington, D.C.: GPO.

U.S. Bureau of Labor Statistics. 1993. *Employment and Earnings,* January.

U.S. Council of Economic Advisers. 1964, 1965, 1967, 1982, 1990, 1993, 1994. *Economic Report of the President.*

U.S. Department of Education, Office of Educational Research and Improvement. 1993. *America's High School Sophomores: A Ten-Year Comparison.* Washington, D.C.: National Center for Education Statistics.

U.S. Department of Health and Human Services, Social Security Administration. 1991. *Social Security Bulletin, Annual Statistics Supplement, 1991.*

U.S. General Accounting Office. 1984. *An Evaluation of the 1982 AFDC Changes: Initial Analyses.*

U.S. House of Representatives, Committee on Ways and Means. 1984. *Effects of the Omnibus Budget Reconciliation Act of 1981 (OBRA), Welfare Changes, and the Recession on Poverty.*

—— Committee on Ways and Means. 1991, 1993, 1994. *Overview of Entitlement Programs: Green Book.*

U.S. Treasury Department, Office of Tax Analysis. 1992. "Treasury Reports on Household Income Changes." *Tax Notes,* August 24.

Weaver, Robert K. 1985. "Controlling Entitlements." In Chubb and Peterson, eds., 1985.

Williamson, Jeffrey, and Peter Lindert. 1980. *American Inequality: A Macroeconomic History.* New York: Academic Press.

Wolff, Edward N. 1992. "Changing Inequality of Wealth." *American Economic Review* 82 (May): 552–558.

Index